Design *as* Activism

September 13–14, 2024
Symposium Proceedings

Institute of Design
at Illinois Tech

ORO
EDITIONS

Publishers of Architecture, Art, and Design
Gordon Goff: Publisher

www.oroeditions.com
info@oroeditions.com

Published by ORO Editions

Editor: Jessica Meharry
Book Design: Jessica Meharry
ORO Managing Editor: Jake Anderson

10 9 8 7 6 5 4 3 2 1 First Edition

ISBN: 978-1-966515-46-3

Color Separations and Printing: Smartpress
Printed in Chanhassen, MN.

International Distribution: www.oroeditions.com/distribution

ORO Editions makes a continuous effort to minimize the overall carbon footprint of its pub-lications. As part of this goal, ORO Editions, in association with Global ReLeaf, arranges to plant trees to replace those used in the manufacturing of the paper produced for its books. Global ReLeaf is an international campaign run by American Forests, one of the world's oldest nonprofit conservation organizations. Global ReLeaf is American Forests' education and action program that helps individuals, organizations, agencies, and corporations improve the local and global environment by planting and caring for trees.

CONTENTS

PROJECT LEADS

Jessica Meharry, Visiting Assistant Professor, Institute of Design at Illinois Tech
Rebecca Beltrán, PhD Researcher, Institute of Design at Illinois Tech
Flora Massah (MDes 2024), Institute of Design at Illinois Tech

STUDENT VOLUNTEERS

Asawer Ahyad
Arundhuti Bhattacharya
Faysal Biobaku
Salena Burke
Avani Chaturvedi
Regina Ellis
Aimee Feuser
Roger Hong
Xuci Hu
Sheethal Jacob
Anushree Joshi
Funmilayo Makinde
Shreya Mathur

Natthaporn (Nand)
 Naktnasukanjn
Ean Neyrey
Meghna Prakash
Kulwadee (June)
 Pruksananonda
Carlos Rodriguez
Rhea Shah
Daniela Vélez
Pratyusha Vellala
Yanting Wang
Shimama Zainab

PHOTOGRAPHY

Dan Chichester
Robbie King

GRAPHIC DESIGN

Jessica Meharry

For more information about the Symposium, including speaker bios, visit:
id.iit.edu/design-as-activism

Design as Activism is part of Art Design Chicago, a citywide collaboration initiated by the Terra Foundation for American Art that highlights the city's artistic heritage and creative communities.

Design as Activism is funded by the Terra Foundation for American Art in connection with the Chicago History Museum's *Designing for Change: Chicago Protest Art in the 1960s-70s.*

ART DESIGN CHICAGO

TERRA
FOUNDATION FOR AMERICAN ART

INSTITUTE OF DESIGN   ILLINOIS TECH

Institute of Design (ID) at Illinois Tech
3137 South Federal Street
Chicago, IL 60616

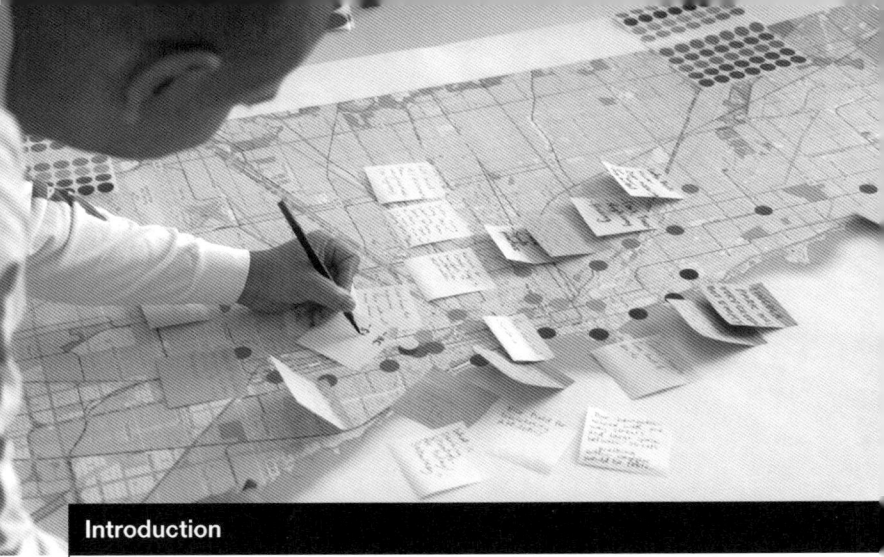

Introduction

Rebecca Beltrán, PhD Researcher, Institute of Design
Flora Massah (MDes 2024), Institute of Design

The Design as Activism Symposium was held on September 13 and 14, 2024 at locations throughout Chicago.

These proceedings capture the key moments and learnings from the *Design as Activism Symposium*. Over the course of two days, attendees engaged with a variety of activations, workshops, and discussions guided by values-driven design, reflecting a wide spectrum of actionable strategies happening right here in Chicago. These conversations not only brought together field practitioners, but designers fueled by a moral imperative—a recognition that design can either reinforce existing inequities or help dismantle them.

As design students, we are guided by our freedom to question and experiment within the context of a learning space. Yet the current political conditions—from fear-based tactics amid growing polarization to widening censorship—pose a serious threat to open dialogue and creative thinking.

Amidst this pervasive political and social uncertainty, these proceedings feel particularly important. Repeated attacks on our democracy and civil society at large remind us that designers have a never-ending responsibility to respond to our biggest challenges in the here and now.

These proceedings feature excerpts from our recorded transcripts of the event. Please take what you need from these conversations. We hope that they inspire you to move past neutrality and make intentional design decisions that can be carried out through even the smallest of actions. By gathering these voices in the field, we invite you to join us in our commitment towards ongoing dialogue and action in strengthening our collective imagination for a just and equitable future. ∎

Opening Remarks

Jessica Meharry, Visiting Assistant Professor, Institute of Design

Chicago has a deep history of designers and artists activating for change. As calls for racial justice, climate action, and gender equity—and more specifically, defunding, disinvestment, and ceasefires—grow louder and more urgent, designers and makers in Chicago demonstrate how design can challenge inequities and systemic oppression. The *Design as Activism Symposium* brings together people currently working to change conditions in their local contexts, from activist strategies serving organizations and corporate clients to more radical forms of disruption.

The symposium is intended to serve as a counterpart to an exhibition currently on display at the Chicago History Museum, *Designing for Change: Chicago Protest Art in the 1960s-70s*. Both that exhibition and this event are supported by grants from the Terra Foundation as part of its Art Design Chicago initiative. The interactive museum exhibit highlights histories of art and design activism in Chicago, beginning with the Chicago Freedom Movement and then exploring the Black Power, women's liberation, anti-war, and gay rights movements. It tells the story of how artists and designers collectively mobilized to call attention to a range of intersectional issues related to labor, race, anti-war, environment, sexuality, gender, and housing. While the *Designing for Change* exhibition explores historical efforts, *Design as Activism* explores the present. How are people working and activating now?

The first day of the symposium featured activations across the city, including a healing session, workshop on craftivism, tour of the exhibit at the Chicago History Museum, tour of the *Voices Embodied* exhibit at the Design Museum of Chicago, the debut of Red Line Service's large-scale 12-foot puppet of care, and a community reading and workshop focused on environmental justice in everyday life.

In addition to the connections we're making to the museum exhibit, we think of this *Design as Activism* event as one of many in an ongoing conversation about designers activating for change. Within the past year alone in Chicago, this includes the *Deem Symposium*, the *Association for Community Design Annual Conference*, and *The Design Summit for Friends of Friends*. In other words, we didn't start this conversation, and it doesn't stop here.

Many of us are passionate about practicing design in a way that promotes equality, inclusivity, and sustainability, but often find ourselves unsure of the practical steps to take. Our goal was to add to this conversation by creating a highly interactive event that focuses on actionable methods that you can think through, try out, and transfer to your own work and strategies. We have invited designers and those who act in designerly ways to share transferable design strategies and methods for generating and impacting change in their communities. To further situate you in context, I have three points to make before you move into your day.

Design as activism: First, I will describe the framing through our symposium title: *Design as Activism*. The word activism comes from the Latin word *actus*: "a doing, a driving force, or an impulse." In many ways, this is perfectly suited for design.

We understand design as *activism*: as taking action, putting theory into practice, and learning through doing and making.

Yet design is also deeply entangled with capitalist systems, with many designers working in service of clients that prioritize profit, growth, and extraction. What space is there for activism, for social and political change within those contexts?

Angela Davis is often quoted as talking about how the word *radical* means "grasping something at the root." The interventions we will talk about today occur at all levels, across a spectrum of engagement and impact. Some are directly grasping for the root, while others may not have access to the root. Some of us are working on large-scale projects, while others are working on small or even micro-projects that remain entangled in larger social and political contexts.

And of course, not all designers think or act this way. We'll talk about the range of approaches and how many of the things we discuss here today intentionally disrupt mainstream design practice and orientations. But no matter the project or the site of intervention, the people we've invited to speak understand the root itself—the systemic structures that hold power and oppression in place.

Positionality: Second, as we talk about activating for social and political change, we also have to pay attention to the specific roles that we—as designers—play and how those roles are shaped by our positionalities and accountabilities.

Design activists must consider how we do or don't reinforce power differentials. This includes how we engage with conflict and dissensus versus consensus and collaboration.

These questions are inextricably bound up with our identities, which are not actually fixed, but change as context changes. For me—a white, cisgender, non-disabled, queer woman who was born in the United States—this attention to power and positionality requires a reflexive design practice that includes continual learning, reflection, and ethical deliberation. But that's me. I look forward to hearing from our speakers and talking with all of you about how *you* think about this in your own practices and activism.

Who we invited: Third, with all of this in mind, I'll describe what our small-but-mighty planning team thought about when gathering this fantastic group of presenters together. We centered an expansive, pluralistic approach that brings together people you may be familiar with, as well as some newer voices and voices outside the design community. When we initially reached out to people, we asked them both if they would be interested in participating and who else they thought we should talk to. Therefore, many of the speakers you will see here today are here because of the networks of collaboration in Chicago, a clear theme that will run throughout the day.

That said, this is not a homogeneous group. You all possess diverse mindsets, orientations, and intentions. You are focused on a range of issues and contexts, and you employ different methods in your work. Today we'll see people describe their work in different ways, including: design justice, participatory design, inclusive design pedagogy, non-western design, matriarchal design futures, reparative futures, multicontextual design, anti-racist design, and trauma-responsive design. These approaches span different applications and forms: built environments, visual communication, placemaking and activating space, building community, connecting to/with/for community, commercial client work, civic efforts, and protests.

Even with our goal to be as inclusive as possible, we know that there are orientations and contexts that aren't represented here today. We know we've unintentionally overlooked some people, and others were invited yet unavailable. But again, this conversation is ongoing. I am excited about the potential of future conversations and collective action around indigenous approaches to design, queering design, and design against fascism, just to name a few. In fact, we have some interactive spaces set up where you all can generate these ideas for future actions together. What's happening now in Chicago, and where do we see this going? How do we get there?

Overall, our goal is to unite designers who practice activism in diverse and innovative ways, all driven by the common purpose of creating a more just and equitable world. We envision this as a platform for mutual learning and a catalyst for ongoing dialogue and collaboration. Again, thank you for coming and making this symposium a reality. I am so glad you are here, and I'm so excited for the day. Let's begin! ■

KEYNOTE

"I'm Not Really Political": Activating Designers in the Work of Sustaining Democracy

Anne H. Berry, Director, School of Design, University of
  Illinois Chicago

In politically fraught climates, engaging designers in conversations about the role of government in society can be daunting. And yet, whether or not we choose to participate in political action or political discourse, politics is still embedded in our everyday lives. From the Voting Rights Act of 1965 to the Americans with Disabilities Act, design and communication are inextricably linked to democracy. This presentation served as an entry point for discussion about the responsibilities that even the most politically reluctant designers among us carry in order to help maintain a healthy democracy.

Anne: I'm going to ask all of you to think about this question: If you had to define yourself politically, what would that look like? I'm not just talking about Republican, Democrat, or Independent.

If you think about the things or experiences in your life that have influenced you, that have changed you, how are those are tied to politics or democracy?

One of the reasons I'm posing this question is because—as a Black woman in the United States—I've had many, many, many conversations about what it means to be a mixed-race person in the United States. I've also had many conversations about my identity as a designer. So it's an interesting question to think about.

Loving v. Virginia

Brown v. Board of Education

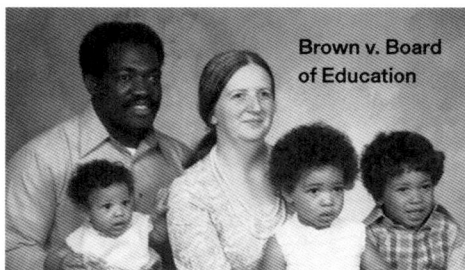

My dad went to a segregated school in the South. My mom grew up in the Midwest. She's holding a snake in this photo on screen, which is interesting—knowing her, I still can't believe that she actually did this! Down in the left-hand corner, there's text that reads *Loving vs. Virginia*. That Supreme Court case was decided in 1967, two years before my parents got married. So when we talk about history, it's important to recognize that for some people, "history" isn't that long ago.

We're a family of educators, and education was really held up as something that was very valued in our home. Some of the things that my siblings and I have been able to accomplish would not have been possible without *Brown vs. Board of Education*. I've just given you two specific examples of ways in which legislation—the laws in this country—have had an impact on me and my family.

Anne's suggestions of people to check out who are working on disability and design:

Jen White-Johnson
Josh Halstead
Elizabeth Guffey

How do we make sure that the things we care about are prioritized? We do that as citizens, as people who are active in our communities, but we also do that by voting. Democracy is government *by* the people. That means us. That means we have a responsibility. Whether we're designers or not, we have a responsibility. The question becomes, how do we invite people who are maybe on the fringes of some of these conversations into the fold, especially other creatives, other designers? What is our responsibility? What is our role in this instance?

Working with students, I've started the conversation by asking them what they care about. Do they care about health insurance? Do they care about being able to use resources at the public library? Do they like being able to take public transportation? Do they care about the environment? From there, we have some nuanced conversations about how we advocate for the things that are important to us. We live in a political system, and change is not going to happen because we have lots of conversations about our priorities. There has to be political will in order to make change happen. That's part and parcel of what it means to live in a democracy. We have to be engaged. It's not a privilege, it's an expectation.

There are many ways in which design has been a contributor to racism and bigotry and negatively affected people's lives. So part of our work is to recognize the ways in which these problematic histories and relationships exist, whether or not we're choosing to identify or acknowledge them. You can stand at a distance, say that you aren't political, and remain reticent about engaging with politics, but that's just now how our society works. I don't think it's a reflection of reality.

Designers need to be ready to push back, stand our ground, and say, "No, we're not going to do that." We just can't afford to be silent. There's nothing neutral about design. Ever.

Whoever you are and wherever you're coming from, you're bringing something valuable to the work that you're doing. Design is still coming *from* somewhere. Somebody created it. Somebody designed it. We can never be fully neutral in anything that we do. ■

IRA vs. Black Lives
© Anne H. Berry
from *Ongoing Matter: Democracy, Design, and the Mueller Report*

How To Share Your Power: A Conversation About Co-Design

Facilitator: Sara Cantor, Co-Founder and Co-Executive Director,
  Greater Good Studio
Nicole Robinson, Chief Executive Officer, YWCA Metropolitan Chicago
Ahmad Jitan, Director of Organizing and Advocacy, IMAN
  (Inner-City Muslim Action Network)
Lesley Kennedy, Director of Strategy and Organizational Development,
  Chicago South Side Birth Center

Despite consensus on the need to redistribute power for equity, it's rarely practiced. This panel with local non-profit leaders explored co-design frameworks, barriers, and strategies for shifting power.

Sara: We're going to start with a shared definition of power. I think of power as the ability to change someone else's reality, or maybe even your own. While power can sometimes feel icky in our culture—and it does get a bad rap because of how often it's abused—at a fundamental level, power is neither good nor bad. It just is, and in fact, it's really important. We can't shy away from power if we want to talk about social change.

So who has power? One way we can think about this is organized people and organized money. Institutions like businesses and government hold power, as do grassroots movements. All of us have some power, at least over some aspects of our own realities.

But as I'm sure we all are keenly aware, power is unequally distributed in our society. So we think about an intervention. At a very high level, for equitable social change, it would seem that we need to see a redistribution of power.

Design is the tangible realization of intent. It's taking our intentions, our goals, and it's turning them into something tangible, something that may change someone else's reality. Design holds inherent power.

Another way to think about design is that it's a structured process of making decisions. Designers work with clients and stakeholders. We facilitate a whole series of decisions. What problem should we solve? Who should we learn from? What did we learn? What are we going to do about it?

By moving our clients through the series of decisions, we're generating a sort of power. Not only that, as designers, we have the ability to extend power to others through our projects. This might be kind of a cheeky way to say it, or a little bit goofy, but I think about co-design as extending the decision-making power of design beyond the client, beyond who's paying you. It's bringing others into the process in order to, number one, make the design itself better, and number two, redistribute some of the power that's been concentrated in the designer-client relationship.

At Greater Good Studio, we bring aspects of co-design and the redistribution of power into every project. Our clients are already on the same page with us, they are all working for an equitable society. And yet, in the 13 years since we've started the studio, I've noticed some barriers that get in the way of

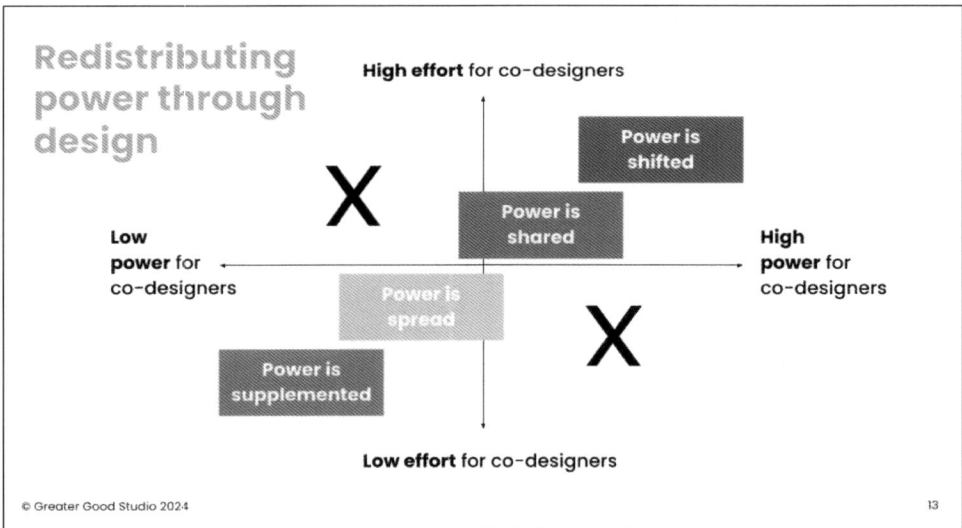

"Redistributing power through design" slide © Greater Good Studio
Sara: "None of these types of power sharing are good or bad, better or worse. We design a project to meet the client's needs while responding to the interests and capacities of the people we're working with... Lots of power with little effort sounds great, but we've never been able to pull that off. And a lot of work for little control would be exploitation."

that redistribution of power which we all claim to want. So I've put together a short list of barriers to co-design:

Emotional barriers	Logistical barriers
• Denial	• Compensation
• "Quality"	• Timing
• Insecurity	• Technology

Some of these are more emotional. Some of these are more logistical. I think they are all swept up in each other.

Sara: None of us is always powerful or always powerless, but we kind of go back and forth in these moments and day to day.

Ahmad: One of the things that the system does that is very effective—because of this capitalist structure, scarcity mindset, and the unhealed trauma across communities—is that it pits communities against each other. So for me, that's one of the ways that where the power is shared.

How do we tackle the issue of food justice and community safety in our neighborhoods? How am I accountable? How am I holding my community accountable to these issues and have been able to build up to the point of having a network of these stores like the GGOR Community Fresh Market that are committed to it? At the same time, how are we recognizing that we're still hitting a wall because of the generations of disinvestment and racism and those obstacles that are there?

As we know, power concedes nothing without a demand. That requires collectivizing and making that demand very clear.

It's those very concrete campaigns. It can start even just at one intersection of being able to see what's actually a problem and be able to shift that.

Further Reading:

The Four Pivots: Reimagining Justice, Reimagining Ourselves by Shawn A. Ginwright

And this pivot—for those familiar with The Four Pivots—can be turning a problem into an opportunity. This problem of Black-Brown tension is actually opportunity for Black-Brown solidarity to build a neighborhood with the people in mind.

Lesley: Similarly with the maternal health crisis that we are in and have been in for a really long time, folks are starting to really wake up. Women, particularly Black women, are giving voice to their experiences. There was a law that wouldn't extend the ability to build a birth center on the South Side. That law had to change. Collectively we strengthened the understanding of folks who may not even feel like they're in that political mindset, or maybe feel powerless that they could change the law, to be able to cultivate the vision to create a different option for women, particularly Black women on the South Side. So now we've moved from the visionary space to the built environment, with an understanding that design coincides with vision, boots on the ground, changing laws, and being able to support folks to feel powerful enough to do that.

Nicole: In my work, power sits with the 90 percent of Black and Brown women who either lead their own home-based childcare or have a community-based childcare center. Because that's a choice point. At the YWCA, we could say we're going to run childcare centers. Instead, we said, "Nope, we're actually going to empower the women who do the work every day." There's not one power point to me, there are multiple power points.

To me, it's all these nuggets of power. It's like when Black and Brown women have ownership, when they grow their own business. That's unleashing power because they actually don't need us to win completely. It's rooted in their own they've created something for themselves and for their families. For example, there's a lot of criticism of public housing, but when we critique things, we can't forget that people are there. How do we give them power? Because actually ignoring people—looking away—is stripping people of power.

Sara: There's always going to be someone who is going to try to cling to their power, because it's the unnamed thing that everybody is trying to get in our culture. But a choice is whether to go *around* that person or to go *through* and say, "You know, if you bring others in, it actually makes you look good. It actually makes you more powerful, because now you have more people on your team."

Nicole: I believe in an inside game and an outside game right now. I do think it is, 'start your own.' It is 'build a coalition.' It is 'work within institutions that are still here.' Part of me is like, yes, just share the power, but we're human beings, and we're in this legacy of domination. So do we walk away from things we should have?

I don't want us to completely walk away. I want us to make our own, build a coalition, and then also keep talking and listening. Let's not be completely polarized.

Ahmad: At the end of the day, the thing that I remind myself, even in our organization, is that I don't need to be the voice for the voiceless. You just pass the mic. That's where, at its base, it becomes a values conversation. You need to be able to clarify your values and then the actual, tangible processes and bodies that you are creating. You need to be able to hold that and live into those values. ■

Just Transition Visioning Project: Building Collaborative Community Processes

Ashley Williams, Executive Director, Just Transition Northwest Indiana
William Estrada, Multidisciplinary Artist and Educator
Kaitlyn Stancy, Visiting Assistant Professor of Graphic Design, Indiana University Northwest

Panelists shared insights from The Visioning Project, which uses art workshops and visionary activities to imagine a Just Transition for the region. They discussed how communities can move toward a regenerative, pollution-free future.

Ashley: Just Transition Northwest Indiana is a grassroots environmental justice organization that came about through a local fight where we were trying to sound the alarms about a silent crisis on the shores of Lake Michigan. This crisis is coal ash waste—two million tons as we speak—that is currently leaking into Lake Michigan. So, we got activated and formed JTNWI because no one else is going to save us. We got organized. We came together. JTNWI is rooted in the Just Transition framework. We live in a sacrifice zone, and on these shores, nearly 50 miles of shoreline are checkered with a panorama of toxic industry.

In Chicago, there's this shared injustice that we have with a corridor of toxic pollution. Communities are being sacrificed for the profit motive. We call this the extractive economy.

Through our organizing, we've been trying to chip away at the pillars of the extractive economy. For us, within a few different fights, art is at the center and informs all of them.

The No False Solutions Campaign is a current campaign that we have been really active around. We are trying to stop BP Whiting from capturing its carbon and pollution and pumping it underground through our communities. This essentially creates a carbon dioxide graveyard that we feel is a ticking time bomb. We call this a *false solution*, and it has no place in a just transition to a regenerative economy.

How are we building solidarity? How are we advocating for communities to be able to get their power back and be at the forefront of decision-making? That's what it's all about: shifting those pillars of power into the hands of the front lines. A Just Transition is s a step towards building the regenerative economy, a visionary framework imagining that just futures are possible, and that a new world is possible.

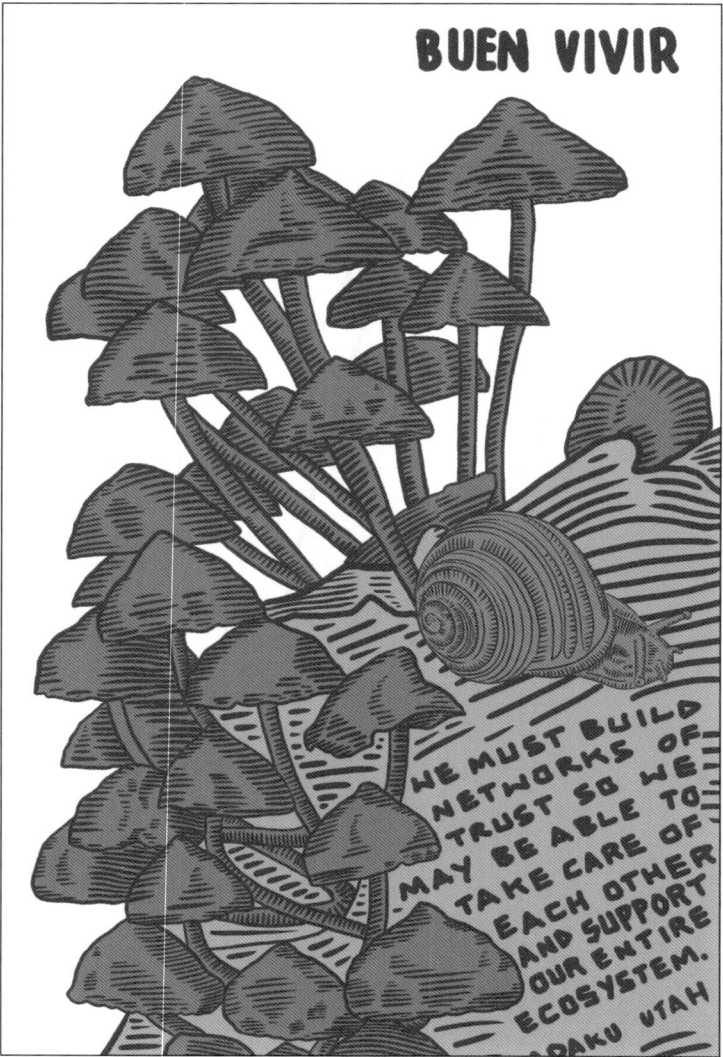

For more information on the Just Transition Visioning Project:
jtnwi.org/visioning-project

Buen Vivir
© William Estrada

A big goal of our work is to create a dynamic space for artists to share, dream, and connect with community organizations. We want to be able to host additional visionary activities and continue talking about the framework. How do we build those intersections with artists and communities in such a way that is unlike anything that we've been able to do before in Northwest Indiana, a historic sacrifice zone?

William: A lot of the work that I've been doing has originated with my own experience growing up. I was born in Southern California and grew up in Mexico, the state of Jalisco. When I was about nine or ten, we came to Chicago, and I've lived across seven different neighborhoods in the South and Southwest Side of Chicago. Earlier today I was in another workshop and folks asked, "What is home?" I have a complicated relationship with that. I'm from a family that had a mixed status. Multiple family members were undocumented, so there were a lot of conversations around where we belonged and where we didn't.

I feel that I'm still becoming critically aware of the intersections of our experiences and the historical aspects that have shaped the way that we see ourselves, the way that resources are present in our community. Or the way that communities have been historically robbed of resources, and then we've been blamed for not having resources.

A lot of the conversations that we started having through Just Transition was thinking about: How do we start engaging as artists? How do we start engaging with concepts that we are still familiarizing ourselves with? How do we engage in the difficult conversations that we need to have in order to explore our own biases?

What are the preconceived notions that we have about communities and our role as artists in either creating culture or maintaining power structures that are harmful to us?

Capitalism has forced many communities to sacrifice culture and tradition for economic survival. Thinking about my own childhood, there are things that I had to sacrifice of myself, of my identity, in order to assimilate and be an "American." In the erasing of our cultures, we're also erasing a big part of our identity and a big part of what makes this nation. It is only through the embrace and respect of our culture and tradition that we can become a whole nation with equitable redistribution of resources and power, where we must work to build new systems that are good for all people and not just a few.

Instead of seeing the land as something we extract from, let's think about the balance that we have between the land and the spaces that we live in and our relationship to them. Our self-determination. All peoples have the right to participate in decisions that impact their lives. This requires democratic governance in our communities, and as we're having a lot of conversations around democracy right now, especially in relationship to the elections, really thinking about an actual democracy, where the people's rights are respected, where people across class and across economic spaces are listened to and are provided with resources to not only live full lives, but also experience joy.

What does solidarity look like in order for us to actually break down walls and think through the spaces that we need to build?

Kaitlyn: I truly believe in the power of art and design to make a difference in our world in our daily lives, even if that is just getting the conversation started and getting the door open so that we can start talking, meeting the right people, and working with the right organizations.

Some of the first steps we need to do for analyzing what's going on with all of these issues is to refuse the way that we're doing it. Let's rethink this and figure out a better way. In one piece of my art, I chose to incorporate a sunflower for this principle. Not only is it beautiful and amazing for our pollinator friends, but it's an extremely regenerative plant that can help sequester carbon and enrich and remediate soil health. They also have super powerful medicinal uses and contain fighter remediation properties that help remove hazardous substances like heavy metals and radiation from contaminated soil. Every little bit helps right now. ∎

RETHINK
REDUCE
REUSE
REPAIR
REFURBISH
REMANUFACTURE
REPURPOSE

Artwork © Kaitlyn Stancy

PANEL

Collaboration Across Collective Networks

Facilitator: Summer Coleman, Design Director and Owner, Severe Side
    Productions LLC
Cecilia Cuff, CEO, The Nascent Group
Dave Pabellon, Associate Professor, Columbia College Chicago
Nick Adam, Associate Partner and Design Director, Span

How does activism in design take root, and what can it grow? These panelists delved into how diverse social environments and actions from their youth shape their lives and design practices. These practices not only reflect their personal values but also actively engage with and uplift the communities they love.

Summer: Can you tell us some challenges that you come up against when trying to collaborate with networks, bring people together, or convey ideas across different platforms?

Nick: Working across networks is powerful, and bringing people into the design process can help level the playing field. When done well, this work engages people who may not have had access to designers and are understandably unsure of what they need or how to participate. While this can extend a project's timeline, a slower, more generous process often yields richer outcomes. A collaborative designer's role must include guiding people to engage and participate meaningfully.

Cecilia: When you design something for other people or for a client, you're applying a value for it. People have an idea of where they're going—from A to Z—and a lot of times, I don't think that design is always a step in that map. Being able to articulate the importance of design to clients is a challenge. Being able to allocate pre-development dollars to any project that you're going to design—if it's a physical project—is an important part of that journey.

It's something that most business owners skip over because they just think of what the end result is going to be.

Dave: I'm kind of going the opposite route. How can I use my creative and scholarly practice to work with people that I really care about and projects that I really align with, to promote their work and use design practice as more or less a full service, where it's not so much capital-based? It's much more about an "effort and amplify" application.

Nick: In the early stages—before work officially begins or a contract is in place—the client often has a range of ideas, some of which could benefit from a "What if we tried this?" or "What if we also considered this angle?" approach. During this time, you're getting to know each other, defining services, and outlining the scope of work. You're also identifying potential pitfalls, like how one idea might negatively impact other aspects of the project. This phase presents a valuable opportunity to reframe the brief, refine the proposal, and shape the direction of the work. And yet, all of this is typically done without compensation.

Summer: How do you see your design journey including more social impact as it pertains to design activism?

Dave: The word *activism* is kind of loaded in a lot of ways, so sometimes it sounds militant. I think about this in a lot of different ways. When we talk about activism, we talk about connectivity, we talk about community. I've known Nick since I moved back to Chicago. I've known CeCe from many circles, personally and professionally, all these things with all these people. I see the Stevenson brothers in the crowd—I have a history with them. I have trust in who they are as people, and I have trust in the way they carry themselves as creatives and community builders.

The thing that creates the thread for me is building an ecosystem or stratosphere of trust, where every person that I work with is somebody I love in some way. Building those relationships is how you figure it out.

Nick: I struggle with the word *activist* because, in many ways, everyone is an activist—it just depends on what they're activating and working toward. I often reflect on how I spend my time and energy because the work I do and the choices I make define the kind of designer I am. Through both my life and my work, I support communities and initiatives I believe in. Because of this, some might label me an activist designer. But consider this: if another designer were up here talking about the incredible work they do for, say, grape soda or social media, no one would call that activism. And yet, it is—it's activism on behalf of sugary pop and tech giants. We all need to examine where we invest our actions, because in the end, that's what defines who we are.

Cecilia: In my eyes, there are so many different types of activists. I have friends who are marching every day. And I have friends who are lobbyists, lobbying for certain causes.

In my role in design, the idea of activism is doing something to influence a group of people to have a different viewpoint.

Cecilia's list of local organizations that blend design and equity in transformative ways:

Revival Arts Collective
revivalartscollective.com

Chicago Freedom School
chicagofreedomschool.org

National Public Housing Museum (NPHM)
nphm.org

Part of my activism is understanding what those systems are that other people are taking advantage of—and not in a bad way. I want to use those same resources used by other companies that don't have the best interest of our community in mind. I want to take advantage of those same resources and bring those resources back to a community, back to something that's more grassroots.

So when I think about activism and my role in activism and in the design that I do, part of the challenge is we have to know that what we're convincing people of we can actually do and figuring out a way to articulate that. Because we are the best advocates for our community. That's a big part of activism.

Nick: There's something interesting emerging across all these stories that I'm just starting to notice—we're talking a lot about conversation and listening. When most people think about design, they focus on what is made or the act of making. But in reality, that's maybe 15 percent of design. The real work happens in the conversations and actions that shape what ultimately gets made.

I try to show up—a lot. That means my work isn't just about the making of graphic design. I'm constantly supporting my friends, their friends, and the things they're building. And often, through that, I end up connecting with

peers who can be brought into the work in meaningful ways. My life and the way I live often informs the work and opportunities that come to our studio.

Summer: What advice would you give to emerging designers trying to align their work with activism? How would you tell them how to get into this design journey of loving in community as well as providing services for community?

Dave: If you don't look in the mirror and you just keep on following the path, you're going to lose yourself. Internal check-ins are necessary. Just know that you have value in your lived experience, but also know that there's other things you might have to sacrifice along the way to live your truest exemplar of practice and passion. ∎

Editor's note: In the exchanges that we had with Dave, Nick, Summer, and Cecilia about the transcript of their panel discussion, Cecilia wrote this additional comment:

Cecilia: I think of Chicago as a "co-conspirator" in our design activism. Specifically the city's wild energy, its history of activism, and its vibrant, rebellious, and often chaotic spirit have deeply influenced the way we approach design. This feels particularly relevant to the symposium's theme and serves as an inspiring reminder for readers to pause, observe, and draw from the world around them.

Too often, designers (and people in general) get caught up in the rush of output, allowing external pressures or global trends to dictate their creative boundaries. But there's something profoundly radical about grounding ourselves in our local contexts—about letting the immediacy of our surroundings inform and inspire our work. Chicago's unique character has pushed us to think differently, to challenge norms, and to design with both grit and heart.

Generating Community Processes through Participatory Design

Lucía Garcés Dávila, Participatory Design Facilitator and Educator

In this workshop, participants explored a generative theme as part of a critical pedagogy approach, applying visual dialogues and creating a shared language to address cultural, social, and environmental practices.

Note: We weren't able to record Lucía's workshop introduction, so here Lucía offers a recap of the workshop with instructions for the activity.

Lucía: During the workshop that I facilitated, participants generated a story map about a one-day journey through the city of Chicago. They reflected on their own experiences and opened a conversation about how they perceived the different neighborhoods that they passed through and the aspirations, concerns, and obstacles that they identified on their route. This exercise has the objective of identifying a *generative theme* (a concept developed by Paolo Freire), which is a key element for guiding the content of a participatory design program in this workshop.

I am a graphic and industrial designer with more than 15 years of experience. While working in this field, I discovered a participatory approach through collaborating with youth and elders from the Mayan community of X-Yatil, Quintana Roo, Mexico. This experience allowed me to integrate practice methods from participatory design, popular education, and participatory action research. Most importantly, I was able to directly experience the meaning of collaboration as it is practiced traditionally by an Indigenous community. Presently, I am facilitating an environmental justice program with youth from the Chicago Public Schools. Previously, I instructed graduate and undergraduate students at the UIC School of Design.

Popular Education (POP ED)
Paulo Freire (1969)
Brazilian philosopher and educator

The community and facilitators in equal collaboration and dialogue on both sides (Freire 1969)

The process begins with the task of identifying a generative theme

"The generative theme could provoke a critical analysis of the current situation to reflect the aspirations of the community' (Moncayo 2014, 12).
In this way, the concept proposed by Freire relates to the experiences, culture, history and daily life in the communities. These themes could be established according to the participants' interest in their social, cultural and environmental factors.

Paulo Freire's Generative Theme slide © Lucía Garcés Davíla

Activity: Developing a Generative Theme

The objective of this activity is to explore the generative theme by co-creating visual narratives through the construction of a map, which is considered a form of elaborating collective stories around the commons. It mounts a platform that makes visible certain meetings and consensuses without flattening diversity because they are also reflected in the process. Additionally, we use a yarning circle activity that, according to Norman Sheehan, consists of learning how to build a small culture within a room by using images and demonstrating how to work in a group to operate this "culture." Thus, knowledge emerges from group interactions, such as conversations with unseen intelligence. In this way, the participants generate a common visual language that will lead to expressing our narratives and reflecting on our positionality to address the generative theme collectively. ■

Further Reading:

"Indigenous Knowledge and Respectful Design: An Evidence-based Approach" by Norman W. Sheehan

The work of Iconoclasistas at iconoclasistas.net

Action and Knowledge: Breaking the Monopoly with Participatory Action Research by Orlando Fals-Borda and Mohammad Anisur Rahman

Pedagogy of the Oppressed by Paolo Freire

I cannot think for others or without others, nor can others think for me.

— Paulo Freire

WORKSHOP ACTIVITY: Call for action

1. **How does each of us perceive this city where we live?**

   You have been given an anonymous map that we are building to reflect on the aspirations and obstacles that we find in our city.

   Mapping prompts
   - Think about the route you took today, considering the neighborhoods you passed through. What is the first thing you thought of when you passed through these neighborhoods?
   - Each person will choose a different color sticker to show their route and will include Post-it notes with short stories or notes about the different neighborhoods.
   - While thinking about your journey through the city, consider the hopes and concerns that you think are related to social, cultural, or environmental factors.
   - Each person will write down their hopes and concerns using Post-its.
   - Discuss with your group the themes that appear in this reflection in order to identify a common topic or identify common relationships between the different themes.
   - Through consensus and discussion, each group will decide on one theme that interests the majority for this workshop.
   - Each group will have three minutes to explain the topic to the other groups.
   - We will then choose one theme to develop through a visual dialogue activity.

2. **How does each of us visualize the theme that we chose?**

   Yarning circles prompts (Norman W. Sheehan, 2011)
   - In a circle, take a card and write a relevant word about the theme that we chose to develop in this workshop. It is a word that you want to keep with you that represents the theme that we will develop.
   - On the other side of the card, illustrate what your word means without including the written word.

   In a clockwise direction, everyone takes turns with time to:
   - Place your card image side up, always connected to another card on the floor.
   - Speak about your card without saying the word on the card.
   - Observe the image that all the cards form on the floor and reflect about the story that you can tell from it.
   - Select the cards to turn over and read the words out loud.

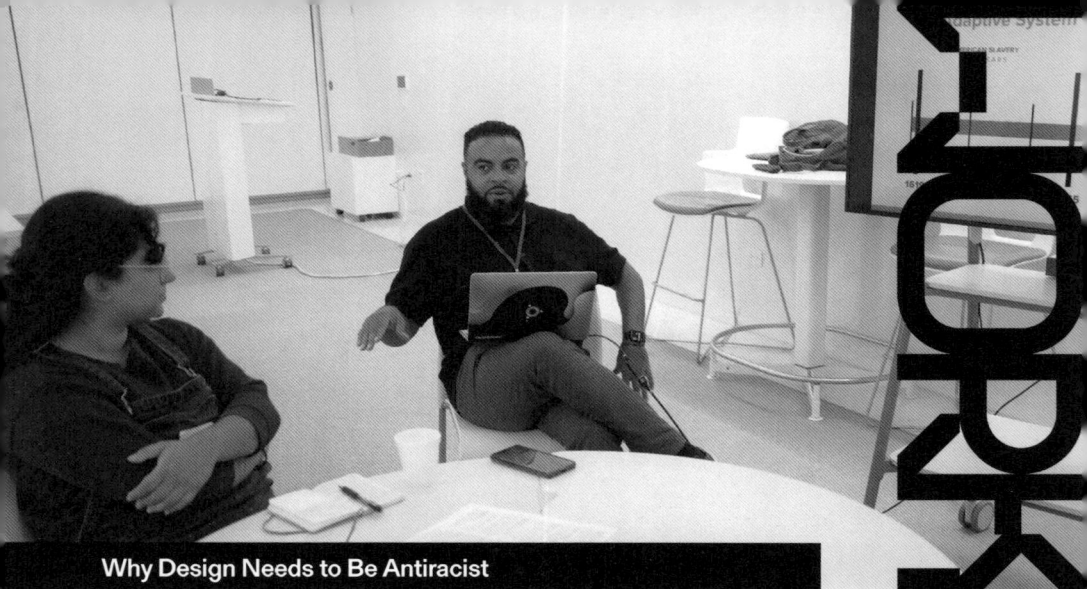

Why Design Needs to Be Antiracist

Chris Rudd, Founder and CEO, ChiByDesign

Design knows very well how to be racist and how to make racism digestible for society. Design has long struggled to get a seat at the table, but how can designers best use that position to serve the underserved and create products and services that are antiracist?

Note: We weren't able to record Chris' workshop introduction, so we are including a portion of the keynote talk he gave at the Institute of Design in 2019 on Community-Empowered Systems Change.

Chris: If we're aiming to redesign systems of governance, then we have to deal with the legacy of slavery and racism in the American context, in Chicago, particularly when dealing with Black communities. In America, we have a long history of perfecting this, the system of exclusion, oppression, and exploitation.

When this country was started, the concept of White was not created yet. When those slave ships started to arrive in 1619, the people who had power, who could make decisions, who could shape this nation, were white men, 21 and older, who owned land and could vote. And they were the ones who could then own property, aka other humans, enslaved Africans. Race was a major technology that they created to sustain this system and allow it to function.

I don't believe that race was created by designers, but it is a design thing. It has changed over time and has adapted to suit the needs of a system that had to separate folks. If we can start to think about race, racism, these historical oppressions, can we now start to think about new ways, new governance structures, new governance systems? I think it is the responsibility of designers to address these historic oppressions in our work toward systems change. If we're not doing that, we're not democratizing the process, we're not addressing the underlying issues that have created the actual scenarios and circumstances in which we find ourselves. Through that, we can empower non-designers to be agents in that change.

A lot of times we use the terms *under-resourced* or *underprivileged* communities when we talk about Black and Brown neighborhoods and the United States. I think that analysis is wrong. I like to say these are *overly exploited* communities. It's not that they don't have those things, it's that there have been targeted interventions or policies to extract from those communities.

The point of view that we have from the beginning is that the system is racist. We have to uncover it and then figure out a solution or solutions. I think we all intrinsically know that oppression exists, but we have to put it at the front of the work. It is what one of the things that we're going to try to solve, and then we can get to more meaningful solutions. ∎

These principles seek to provide a pathway to antiracism for the individual. They should be used in the creation of products, services, strategies, and policies. But this is by no means a complete list. As we continue our design work, more principles will reveal themselves.

1 Challenge the concept of race

To create an antiracist world, we must combat the primary notion that groups of humans are biologically different from one another based on "race."

2 Initiate critical conversations

Designing antiracist outcomes requires us to export the critical conversations that we should be having internally on teams, in the studio, and within companies out to the world through our deliverables (such as strategies, products, and services).

3 Facilitate collective antiracist action

Antiracism requires consistent, explicit, and overt intentionality. In short, antiracism requires collective action.

4 Transfer resources to communities targeted by racism

A key component of antiracist design and difference from equity-centered design is that antiracist design focuses on the redistribution of economic resources, specifically for communities of color, to counteract the generational super-exploitation enacted upon those communities.

Anti-racist principles for designers © Chris Rudd

Matriarchal Design Futures: A Collective Work in Progress

Heather Snyder Quinn, Assistant Professor, DePaul University

What would happen if a matriarchal design pedagogy was considered? What if our patriarchal training was unlearned? What if we abandoned solutionism for unknowing, thereby replacing design for consumption with design for the pluriverse? In this workshop, Heather shared Matriarchal Design Futures, *a non-capitalistic, non-hierarchical framework co-created with Ayako Takase that centers the practices and values of caregiving and nurturing.*

Heather: Our inspiration is not academic; it is through our lived experiences. We want to unlearn the systems and structures under which we've been trained, and we use the word *train* strategically. We love glossaries and revisionist dictionaries, and that was a huge part of this work. We asked people to redefine the definitions on the worksheet you have in front of you. It's the idea that there isn't one definition for one word; there can be multiple definitions. An example is the definition of the word *matriarchal*, which is an imperfect word, but we selected it intentionally for this project to serve as a provocation. There isn't just one future;there can be many.

As artists and designers, we are generally good at imagination and innovation. Yet all the systems and structures are so ingrained in us that it's often hard to imagine things could be different. How do we unsettle the present field? So many times we just accept the status quo. We have to remember there can be another way. This mindset is absolutely critical when doing futures work.

When my creative partner Ayako Takase and I started working and teaching, we talked frequently about the things we were up against. These are things that we saw in our students, that we saw in ourselves, that we wanted to try to minimize or unlearn.

The words on our worksheet come from the communities we've worked with and represent the current state of societal values, many of which work against our best intentions as designers and educators. However, these imagination workshops create a revised and expansive view of teaching and industry work centered around values such as care, joy, ethics, respect, holistic thinking, and intuition. What might that look like more from a societal perspective?

Ayako and I feel that in our teaching and work, if we influence one student, one classroom, and they go out into the workplace, these small ripples make considerable effects over time.

Suppose you teach a student to catch an ethical quandary in an interface design, or you teach them how to lead with care even in difficult situations like terminating an employee. Those actions make a real difference in changing the culture and expectations of a field over time. These small actions are the essence of matriarchal design future values and principles, which are ever-evolving.

The *Matriarchal Design Futures* work intentionally uses a circular motif to reflect continuity, collective learning, and a non-hierarchical approach to design, where everyone is both a teacher and a learner. The circle also carries layered meanings: it represents the nest, the womb, and the earth. In one of our diagrams, we place the values we want to center in the middle while the forces we're working to resist are positioned around the outside. One of those structures is capitalism. It's the system we're currently part of, and for many, especially students, there's no simple way to step outside of it. Most will need to find jobs and begin their careers within existing frameworks. We approach this with awareness. Part of our work is helping students learn how to enter these spaces thoughtfully, carrying with them a different ethos.

"If you want to make change in the world, you have to operate within it."

— Superflux

Superflux London is one of our favorite speculative design studios, and we often return to their quote: "If you want to make change in the world, you have to operate within it." For us, this serves as a reminder to move forward with intention, sometimes in big strides, but more often through steady engagement with the systems we're already part of. It's through this ongoing participation that we recognize, share, model, teach, learn, and influence. In doing so, we gradually become agents of change. These collective principles, embracing the idea of work in progress, challenge the notion that we must be exceptional to be seen or valued. As designers, we're often taught to strive for perfection, but we are trying to unlearn and model that as much as possible.

In leading the next generation, what are our hopes for future designers in the field? How do we foster these qualities? What rules and barriers do we need to remove? What kind of environment do we need to build, rebuild, burn down?

We don't see this work as only incremental—there's room for bold, radical steps, too, and we hope those who take them continue to lead in meaningful ways. At the same time, change doesn't have to be all or nothing. There are many ways to participate and contribute. This work is about making room for people to imagine themselves in any future and to think beyond the limits that shape the present. We often ask: what does it mean to teach with care and joy? What does it look like to move away from elitism, to question perfectionism, and to challenge the idea that only the exceptional are valued? These are the questions that guide our practice. ∎

Conversation sketchnotes © Abigail Auwaerter (MDes 2023)

current social values

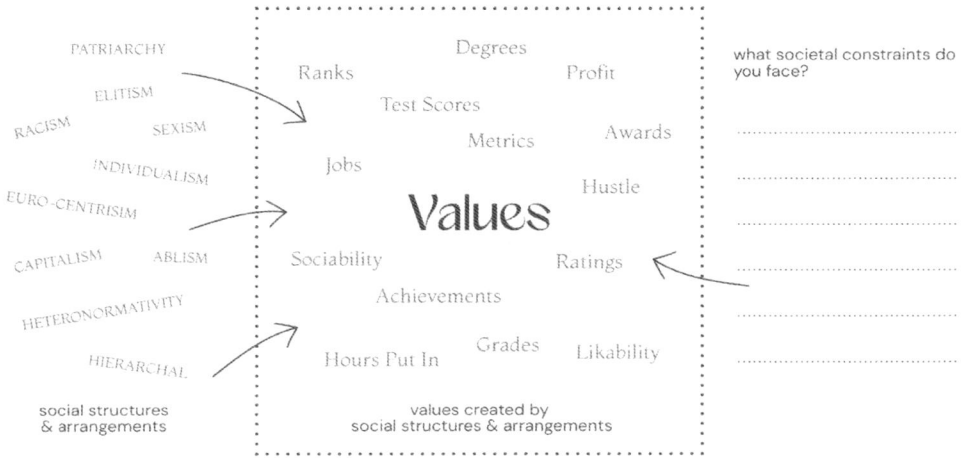

PATRIARCHY

ELITISM

RACISM   SEXISM

INDIVIDUALISM

EURO-CENTRISIM

CAPITALISM   ABLISM

HETERONORMATIVITY

HIERARCHAL

social structures
& arrangements

Ranks   Degrees   Profit

Test Scores

Metrics   Awards

Jobs

Hustle

Values

Sociability   Ratings

Achievements

Grades   Likability

Hours Put In

values created by
social structures & arrangements

what societal constraints do
you face?

....

....

....

....

....

....

matriarchal design futures
values, and principles

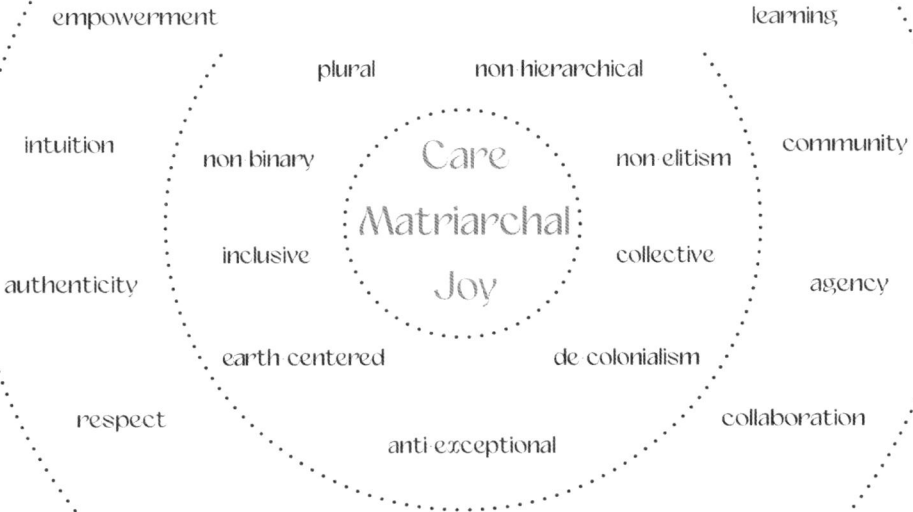

empowerment   learning

plural   non-hierarchical

intuition   community

non-binary   non-elitism

Care
Matriarchal
Joy

inclusive   collective

authenticity   agency

earth-centered   de-colonialism

respect   collaboration

anti-exceptional

Excerpts from *Matriarchal Design Futures: A Collective Work in Progress* © Ayako Takase and Heather Snyder Quinn,
2020-2024

MAPPED: Making a People's Pathway for Engaging Design

Clio Lyons, Operations Manager, Design Trust Chicago
Emma Jasinski, Senior Community Designer, Design Trust Chicago

MAPPED is Chicago's public platform for documenting community projects across the city—built, envisioned, or planned. In this interactive workshop, participants learned how to contribute to this collaborative design library of community visions.

Clio: We work with the city of Chicago on various place-keeping and place-making initiatives, particularly along neighborhood corridors on the Southwest Sides. We engage community leaders directly and help guide them through a preliminary design process to bring their neighborhood visions and various projects to life. We also build tools that help to share design knowledge more broadly with the public. That brings us to the topic of today, which is our MAPPED tool, Making A People's Pathway for Engaging Design, a digital library of community projects across the city.

It operates similarly to Wikipedia in that it's entirely open source, and all the information housed on the platform is user-generated and user-identified. We intend it to be used as a way to highlight works in the built environment that aren't traditionally included in design thought leadership. It can serve as a starting point for future design initiatives, creating a database to help build knowledge around community design and design process at large.

Emma: One of the geneses for creating this was that our three co-founders were engaged in a lot of this work. While they were happy to share it, they were saying, wouldn't it be great to just have a library or a space or a public forum where this information could be accessed? That is at the center of this tool, providing information to our fellow Chicagoans.

We have these six different typologies, starting with *public spaces* such as parks, playgrounds, plazas, anything publicly owned and maintained. The next is *community spaces*, which seem kind of similar, but a community space could be privately owned, with the intention that it is for the public. Or it might be an arts nonprofit, but owned privately. So that's the distinction between those two.

The next is urban design, *urban planning*. That might be like a robust master plan that's envisioned for a specific neighborhood or even the overall city when it comes to transit or maybe waterfront access. Then we have *placemaking*. This includes art markets and murals. Then we have *toolkits or guidelines* around neighborhood corridors or design interventions and things like that. Finally, we have a *research/studies* type feasibility and history reports.

Clio: There are mapping databases similar to this that are a little intimidating and are so granular in the information that they provide. We didn't want that. We didn't want this to be a tool that would scare away an average user, someone that maybe isn't in the design community. We want this to be used across a large variety of communities and networks. ∎

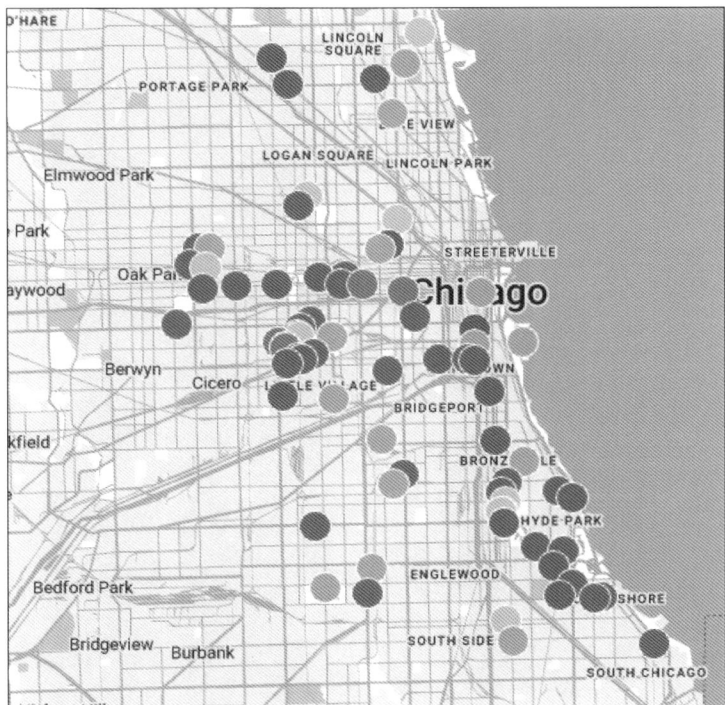

MAPPED Database at www.mappedchicago.org

Reparative Futures Processes for Radically Hopeful Visions

Jessica Meharry, Visiting Assistant Professor, Institute of Design
Hillary Carey, Design Specialist, Just Visions LLC
Luce James, Design Strategist, Ascendant

New paths forward emerge when past injustice is examined to imagine better futures. A reparative futures approach can alter the orientations and methods of anti-oppressive design work and generate a different set of affective, joyful outcomes. In this workshop, we explored how radically hopeful visions created through critically conscious reparative futures practices offer an additional way to engage with reparative processes.

Jessica: Today, we're diving into a futuring activity that takes a reparative approach—one that acknowledges past and present injustices and helps us imagine more just futures. The word *reparative* is connected to reparations, meaning the ways we address and make amends for historical and ongoing harm. As designers committed to anti-oppressive strategies, we believe that understanding how the past and present are connected is essential to shaping the future responsibly. If we don't fully grasp the systemic roots of oppression and injustice, we risk repeating harmful patterns.

The approach we're using today is grounded in anti-racism. Anti-racist work involves reexamining history through a racialized lens, asking: How have past policies and actions shaped today's racial inequities? With that deeper understanding, we can make more intentional choices that repair harm and lead to more equitable outcomes.

Beyond recognizing harm, reparative efforts also uplift histories of activism— stories that remind us that people have always resisted injustice and fought for change. This connects to a broader idea of *historical consciousness,* which researchers use to help organizations rethink their past in order to drive meaningful change.

When organizations challenge a single, dominant narrative of their history, they open up new possibilities for the future. In short, reframing the past creates space for hope and transformation.

Both of these strategies—anti-racism and historical consciousness—are about reframing the past to make space for hope in the present and future. Reframing the past becomes necessary in order to imagine hopeful futures. Shared imagination about the future provides motivation and guidance. Taking inspiration from these re-examinations of histories, we can create future visions to help draw people together toward positive change.

Further Reading:

Emergent Strategy: Shaping Change, Changing Worlds by adrienne maree brown

The Radical Imagination: Social Movement Research in the Age of Austerity by Max Haiven and Alex Khasnabish

Freedom Dreams: The Black Radical Imagination by Robin D.G. Kelley

Utopia as Method: The Imaginary Reconstitution of Society by Ruth Levitas

Imagining the future isn't just about thinking ahead—it's about understanding how the past informs the present. A hopeful future requires us to challenge dominant narratives, surface hidden histories, and engage in collective imagination. When we rethink history, we can build futures that bring people together for real change.

Our Approach: Reparative and Participatory Futures

Our process draws from researchers who work with participatory futures and reparative futures, centering the past as a key part of futures thinking—something that's often missing in mainstream futuring approaches. Our approach includes:

- examining past harms and moments of resistance
- envisioning radically hopeful futures together
- bringing those futures to life through storytelling

To ensure we're fostering justice-based futures, we also focus on:

- including diverse perspectives and lived experiences
- centering different ways of knowing
- empowering people to co-create their own future visions
- collaborating rather than assuming ownership of the process
- drawing on cultural knowledge as a source of inspiration

Additionally, we embrace decolonial futures—a perspective that critiques dominant futuring methods for ignoring the political realities of race, capitalism, patriarchy, and colonialism. We push back against narrow assumptions about:

- what the world looks like today
- how injustice was experienced in the past
- who gets centered in the future
- the idea that time moves linearly from past to present to future

By questioning these dominant frameworks, we create space for more just and imaginative possibilities.

Workshop Activity

Luce: With that background, let's try today's activity. Each group will choose one of these spaces in Chicago: the 'L' Train; a Chicago park; a Chicago beach; or a classroom at Illinois Tech.

As a group, you'll investigate how your space looked and functioned in the past (around 1905), how it functions today in 2024, and imagine what it could look like in the future in 2060.

This workshop is about envisioning positive change, especially for those who've been historically excluded. **How have marginalized groups—those who have been oppressed by race, gender, sexuality, age, ability, and more—experienced and shaped these spaces over time?** ∎

RADICALLY HOPEFUL VISIONS

The setting: 29th Street Beach, Chicago

Lakefront beaches became leisure spots by the late 19th century. However, beaches were segregated and many excluded marginalized communities.

Past: 1905 – Let's start by going back in time to around the year 1905. Picture your chosen place during this period. Using the POEMS framework (below), think about who would have been there. Who was allowed to use the space, and who was excluded?

Present: 2024 – Now, let's fast-forward to today. In the year 2024, how is this space being used? What's changed, and what remains the same? This is your chance to reflect on current realities and the inequalities that still exist in the space.

Future: 2060 – Now for the exciting part—let's leap ahead to the year 2060. Imagine what your space could look like in the future. This is where we'll get creative. We want you to draw that future. **What are the qualities of a radically hopeful vision of a Chicago beach in 2060?**

People: Who is at the beach? Who isn't allowed at the beach? Who wouldn't feel safe at the beach?

Objects: What is on the beach? Are there chairs? Towels? Refreshment stands? Is it accessible?

Environments: What is the atmosphere of the beach? Is it fun? Is it safe? Is it peaceful? What is the current socio-political and environmental context of the space?

Messages: What is the signage on the beach? Are there flags? Are there posters? What were the social messages or laws governing this space? What unspoken norms govern these spaces?

Services: What services are there at the beach? Are there activities? How accessible are the services? Who benefits most?

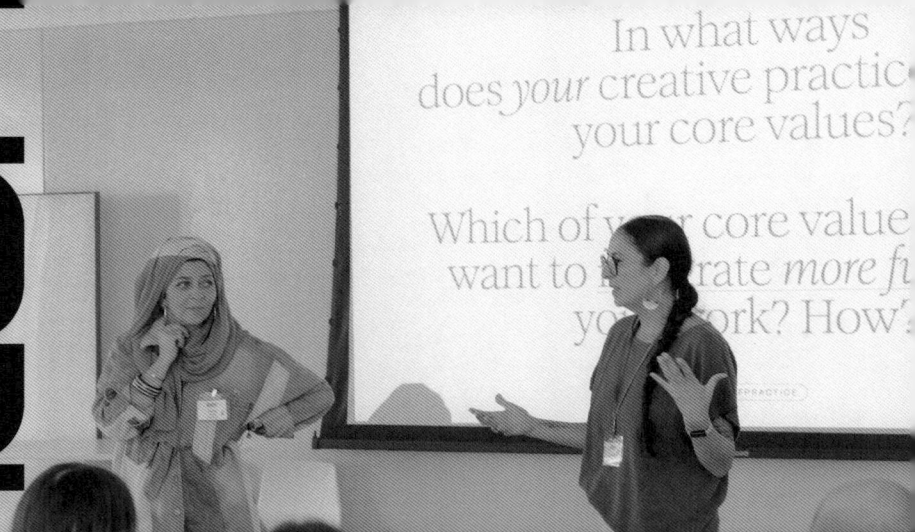

In what ways does *your* creative practic[e] your core values?

Which of y[ou]r core value[s] want to [ce]l[eb]rate *more f[ully]* yo[ur w]ork? How?

Walking the Walk: Define Your Values, Design Your Practice

Nermin Moufti, Co-founder + Design Director, Field of Practice
Kristin Lueke, Co-founder + Strategic Director, Field of Practice

In this interactive session, participants discovered what it means to design for change. They were prompted to reflect on their creative journey, explore shared values, and discuss the challenges and rewards of intentional practice.

Kristin: When we started our business, we treated ourselves as a client and used this core values exercise to help us figure out how we're going to build a business that leveraged our combined skill set and centered our shared values and beliefs.

We started exactly the way that you did today—as individuals, confronting a list of about 140 words, trying to move quickly, trying to move intuitively, not overthink anything. The goal was to find those words in that sheet that felt most alive and energized to us. For instance, the words that came up for me included things like beauty and generosity, dignity and discipline. After I circled everything that was coming to light for me, I crossed out everything else, anything that didn't feel as critical or as important. As I mentioned earlier, you may have noticed missing words. So for me, that meant adding balance, compassion, competence, and grace.

But then the hard part really begins trying to get that big list down to 30, and then cutting that in half. One thing I noticed—maybe some of you did, too—it was easier to let go of some of these values by actually creating more. Subtracting by adding. This is how humility and solidarity came into the mix. For me, this felt super fruitful, super generative. You just have to keep cutting and cutting again, trimming until you get down to about five to seven.

Here's where I landed in 2020: abundance, imagination, integrity, love, transformation, balance, and grace. I wanted to start a business that embraced these values, but of course, I had a business partner. So we smashed our lists together and were able to pretty quickly spot where there was already some super strong alignment, where the heat was, where the energy was, and also some really interesting points of productive tension. For instance, how are we going to find stability and balance while also maintaining flexibility and being nimble? What does it look like to both work with discipline *and* breaks? What we started finding was that we really felt at home in our hearts.

Doing this exercise as a young business really helped us develop a clear set of values and practices that we bring to bear in pretty much all of our business and creative decisions.

Here's where we landed as Field of Practice. We're going to think and do differently. We will choose abundance over scarcity. We are going to agree that we will work together and go farther. And maybe hardest, of all, we are going to try to design without ego. These values really do inform how we work together, how we structure our conversations, our work environment, how we conduct retrospectives amongst ourselves, with our clients, and of course, what work we're going to say yes to. They've influenced every part of our branding and messaging. We can see in here, our lived experiences of change and connection, as well as nourishing sustainable creative partnerships. Defining and aligning our shared values really helps us figure out how to tell our story precisely and clearly, both visually and verbally.

Moving from values into practices—we acknowledge who we are and who we're not. Who we are: two women who are not particularly satisfied with the status quo. If there is an established way of doing things that feels unreasonable to us and inequitable, sexist, or ableist, we really try not to do it that way. It means we have to try very hard to choose progress over perfection and move at the speed of our collective capacity, not a situation where one person sprints out ahead and leaves someone behind and resents them for it. No, we check in with each other. Our ways of work can vary, day to day and week to week. How far can we get this week in everything else that's going on?

And finally, designing without ego is saying, "I don't know" all the time. It means seeking feedback early and often, practicing active listening and presence in every conversation, because we really and truly do believe that the quality of our conversation affects the quality of our work and relationships. All of this thinking, all of this talking that we did around our values also helped us get to a few non-negotiables as a young business.

By adopting these new ways of working and thinking about our work, putting our values front and center, we really have had a chance to work with some extraordinary people and projects.

We want to see all these folks thrive now and in our shared future. The common thread across all of these industries, every client that we take on, is that we all want to design for change. We're hungry to move the needle in our industries and our networks and our households. In our hearts, we do not want a seat at a dysfunctional table. We want to build and move on together.

Nermin: As much as we can, we recognize that saying "I don't know" is half the knowledge. Some of the best work we've done, the most gratifying projects are those that demand that we stretch ourselves beyond our collective limited wisdom and afford us the opportunity to work in co-creation with others who are generous enough to share their own truths and wisdoms.

_____

Sometimes we just trust that inner calling to say yes, trusting in that working together is also a great lesson in letting go of control, knowing that the best work comes from the meshing of the brains. We really need one another to make the work _work_. ∎

WALKING THE WALK — NERMIN MOU FTT / KRISTIN LUEKE

DEFINE YOUR VALUES, DESIGN YOUR PRACTICE

CREATIVE STUDIO

2020

"WORK WAS JUST NOT WORKING FOR US.."

FIELD OF PRACTICE
— WOMEN OWNED

◁ CORE VALUE EXERCISE ▷

MEMBER OWNED COLLECTIVE OWNERSHIP

FINDS THE WORDS THAT RESONATE

WE HAVE TO KNOW WHAT IS IMPORTANT TO US TO MAKE IMPORTANT DECISIONS

WE HAD TO CUT, CUT, CUT

"The World Is Our Field of Practice"

Conversation sketchnotes © Abigail Auwaerter (MDes 2023)

WORKSHOP ACTIVITY: Identifying Your Values

Review the list below and circle each word that resonates with you. Some may be similar—pick whichever feels most alive for you. If you notice something missing, add it to the list.

Abundance	Ecology/Environment	Investing	Resilience
Achievement	Ethics	Joy	Resourcefulness
Activism	Excellence	Justice	Respect
Adventure	Excitement	Kindness	Responsibility
Affluence	Experience	Knowledge	Safety
Approval	Expertise	Leadership	Security
Art	Expressiveness	Learning	Self-Reliance
Beautiful Things	Fairness	Love	Sensuality
Beauty	Faith	Loyalty	Serenity
Belongings	Fame	Making a Difference	Service
Challenges	Family	Mastery	Significance
Change	Financial	Meaningful Work	Simplicity
Clarity	Independence	Mindfulness	Spirituality
Comfort	Fitness	Money	Stability
Commitment	Flexibility	Nature	Status
Community	Freedom	Open-Mindedness	Success
Compassion	Friendship	Order	Teaching
Competence	Frugality	Originality	Thrift
Competition	Fun	Owning	Thriving
Connection	Generosity	Peace	Tradition
Consciousness	Growth	Perfection	Transcendence
Conservation	Happiness	Philanthropy	Transformation
Contentment	Harmony	Play	Trustworthiness
Contribution	Having the Best	Pleasure	Truth
Control	Health	Power	Uniqueness
Country	Helping Others	Privacy	Unity
Creating	Home	Productivity	Virtue
Decisiveness	Honesty	Prosperity	Vision
Devotion	Imagination	Purpose	Wealth
Dignity	Independence	Reason	Wellness
Discipline	Individuality	Recognition	Wisdom
Discovery	Influence	Recreation	Worthiness
Diversity	Innovation	Relationships	_____
Duty	Integrity	Reliability	_____
Education	Intelligence	Religion	_____
Enjoyment	Intimacy	Reputation	_____

Now trim it down to 20-30 words.

Then narrow it down to 10-15.

Keep trimming it down, one word a time, until you're left with 5-7.

These are your core values. Try adding a verb to each one. Take a moment to consider how these values show up for you. What habits and behaviors reflect these values?

Core Values Exercise used by Field of Practice

Designing for Disability at the Intersection of Policy, Built Environment, and Trauma Awareness

Facilitator: Cheryl Dahle, CEO, Flip Labs
Ruth Aguilar, Senior Ligas Family Advocate, The Arc of Illinois
Dimitri Nesbitt, Knowledge Mobilization Specialist, Center for Racial and
  Disability Justice at Northwestern University Pritzker School of Law

Most, if not all, of us will become disabled one day. Despite that near-universal experience, our designers, institutions, and governments do a consistently shabby job anticipating the needs of those with disabilities or even consulting them in the design process. Ableism is deeply embedded in socialization and civic participation and encoded in buildings and services. This panel explored the systemic and cultural issues behind this ongoing injustice, as well as ways that design can lead the way to a more just future.

Cheryl: What are some of the types of gaps that we have in accessibility? What things are terribly designed and present real, structural, and systemic problems for people with disabilities?

Dimitri: I recently heard a CDC recording that said that one in four Americans are disabled. This is one of the biggest minority populations in the United States, and it's one that anyone can fall into at any moment. That's a huge consideration when you are a designer. How do you start visualizing how some of these people go through space and go through their lives and experience a lot of these injustices? A really big way that some of these gaps and some of the social reproduction of injustice occurs is by this very incomplete data set that we have. A lot of designs are informed by data, which also informs urban planning, urban design, and architecture. You study the context areas, you study the site itself and what the existing conditions are, and then you make recommendations based on that.

But the data there at the point of origin of the existing conditions that you're studying is incomplete because people with disabilities are not included. They're not included in the design of the research questions. They're not even included in an intersectional way. Data isn't disaggregated to understand how queer disabled people experience things, versus black disabled people, versus anyone else.

The incompleteness of that data means that you are designing an incomplete world as well. There's an aspect of this that needs to be focused on disability data justice.

There needs to be more of a command of the process to give people with disabilities the opportunity to define for themselves what these questions look like and how we collect data.

Ruth: Judy Heumann, the mother of the disability rights movement, said, "I know discrimination when I see it." Not including people with disabilities or that intersectionality of being gender different with having a disability or the layer of having an accent and having a disability comes with the effect that they are not taking my word into account into those research studies. How you can design something for somebody if you are not listening to their needs, to their opinions, to their likes and wants?

Cheryl: How could design processes be different to include enough voices so that discrimination doesn't happen? What kind of design process, methods, or tools have you seen or used yourself that incorporate these voices in the process?

Dimitri: You have to incorporate a lot of different perspectives. You have to be willing to engage in dialogue with people who are not designers. You also have to be able to communicate design thinking, processes, and techniques to people that are there to provide you feedback. It's about being able to incorporate the perspectives of local people.

This is really kind of the modality that we should be working in when designing and revitalizing a lot of the built environment. In a recent project, we utilized a charrette, which is essentially a co-generated, community-led experience in design. You have a lot of different activities that are helping people visualize the built environment, read it for what it is, and then ultimately make their own determinations about what they

want. This is very exciting because you're getting feedback that is organic and unbiased in a lot of ways, based on the data that you might have as well. That's another way to be able to improve your designs and have other people trust them when they have a stake in it, when they then see themselves represented in it. They see their voice as a part of your conversation and your design process. Ultimately, that makes all of your designs much more fortuitous in a way.

Cheryl: Yes, to highlight some of your points— design, historically, has been a process that has been inculcated in academia and also in corporate settings. Because of that, embedded in design are white dominant values and views about process that are built on white supremacy.

One of design's huge mistakes was to take a corporate model for how to do design research and apply it to community-based research. That kind of research is extractive.

When you talk about co-design, you're talking about something different. What are some of the principles of interacting with people in a community, the disabled community or others, where you're trying to be much more mindful of reciprocity and building a relationship?

Dimitri: In co-generated designing you're building relationships with people where you're actively understanding their point of view, their own stories, and then incorporating that into a design that they also can trust. Sometimes that might be like a relationship where you're offering something back to the community. The reciprocity of maybe a financial restitution of some kind, whether you're paying people for their opinions, hosting an event such as a design charrette and then making sure that they're fed, and providing childcare there for people who need it. A lot of these different things just have to be built into both the budgeting of your designs as well as the actual practice. If you're able to establish in your practice very early on that you want to be able to ensure and trust that your designs will be the best that they can be and include that community aspect, you're set up for more success overall, more chances of being able to do things righteously.

———————————

Cheryl: When thinking about how designers approach projects, we're very good at looking at monetary cost, but we're much less good at looking at the opportunity costs of exclusion and what that means for communities and individuals. Designing for people with disabilities makes things easier

DESIGNING FOR DISABILITY

RUTH AGUILAR

SENIOR LIGAS FAMILY ADVOCATE, THE ARC OF ILLINOIS

I HAVE A DAUGHTER WITH A DISABILITY. I'VE LEARNED TO EMBRACE DISABILITIES, WORKING AND ADVOCATING AT THE STATE LEVEL TO HELP OTHERS HAVE A GREAT QUALITY OF LIFE

CHERYL DAHLE

CEO OF FLIP LABS

I BECAME INTERESTED AS A DESIGNER AS I HAVE AN INVISIBLE DISABILITY. MY FOCUS IS CENTERING COMMUNITIES WITH SYSTEMS DESIGN

1 in 4 AMERICANS HAVE SOME DISABILITIES

WHEN ASK IF THEY SAW MOMENTS OF INJUSTICE...

6%
NON-DISABLED INDIVIDUALS ONLY SAW...

EMPATHY GAP....

BUT

50%
DISABLED INDIVIDUALS SAW!

ADA

ITS A LAW, WE HAVE IT...
BUT ITS **NOT REALLY ENFORCED**
☑ WE'RE JUST TRYING
☑ TO MEET CRITERIA
BUT THATS **NOT HOW PPL. MOVE**

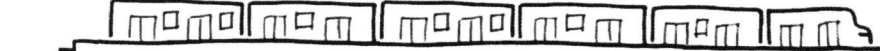

ONLY A HANDFUL OF CTA STATIONS HAVE ELEVATORS — AND CTA HAS INCOMP. DATA ON IT

Conversation sketchnotes © Abigail Auwaerter (MDes 2023)

AT THE INTERSECTION OF POLICY, BUILT ENVIRONMENT, & TRAUMA AWARENESS

ALL OF THESE INSTANCES HAVE AN ARCH. FOUNDATION

WORKING IN KNOWLEDGE MOBILIZATION I STRIVE TO MAKE INFORMATION ACCESSIBLE TO ALL. I ALSO HAVE A BACKGROUND IN BUILT ENVIRON

DIMITRI NESBITT

KNOWLEDGE MOBILIZATION SPECIALIST, CENTER FOR RACIAL & DISABILITY JUSTICE AT NORTHWESTERN UNI. PRITZKER SCHOOL OF LAW

THESE BUILT SPACES — GREAT FOR SOME, HARMFUL FOR OTHERS

for everybody. This is one of the principles of design that we forget about, designing for the extremes. I would love for each of you to just give a couple closing comments. Are there things that I haven't that you want to add?

Ruth: For my closing statement, I want to use two quotes. These are not my words, but I think they are very powerful, and they go hand in hand with what we are talking about today. On July 26, 1990, when the Senate and the House passed the ADA, President Bush signed it and said in part of his speech, "Let the shameful walls of exclusion finally come tumbling down." I want to leave you with the question, if we want to see a better world, what we can do to really remove that wall that we still see in our world? Because that wall still exists. What we can do to remove at least one brick out of that wall?

Dimitri: My parting advice to designers is to always design for multiplicity. Always design for the client that is singularly not you, and that is not your client as well. Understand that your designs will be utilized and occupied by especially built environment designs that are much more permanent in some ways than a lot of others. Designing for multiplicity allows us to be able to consider the temporality of design as well as its use. When designing for disability, there are a lot of obstacles, and you don't want your designs to be one of them for people. ■

Designing for Ourselves: A Conversation on the Impact of Local Design Languages

Facilitator: Amira Hegazy, Adjunct Associate Professor,
  University of Illinois Chicago
Sir Charles, Lettering Artist, Made in Chi Town with Love

Sir Charles uses his lettering work to represent Chicago's South Side neighborhoods with integrity and love. Focusing on localized design, this conversation considered ways that community-built aesthetics can help us directly speak and design messages that are effective and affirming.

Amira: The project that I've been working on at the Design Museum of Chicago is about the typography of Chicago. Often when we think about typography, we think about Oswald Cooper, we think about Caslon and Baskerville, big names in typography. But I was trying to think, what does typography have to do with the way that we actually experience type in the world? How do we talk about the way that people read and understand, how does that shape design, and who designs in these ways?

So I've started to build this project by talking to a lot of different people who make letters. Sometimes the word typography doesn't fit those folks. Like Charlie, his practice is vast and different, and it's not always regular. There are many different styles. I work with sign painters, other graffiti writers, and calligraphers. I've started to understand that the way these people—these designers—design letters and write information changes the way that it's received in huge ways. This is often in ways that some of my design colleagues think is not great. Unfortunately, sometimes they're like, "That's ugly." And I think, maybe it's ugly to you because it's not for you. Maybe they don't want you to know what they're saying. So this work has started to build toward a theory about love as a principle within design and how we can organize around that. Charlie, would you like to introduce yourself?

Charlie: Good morning everybody, my name is Charlie. I also use a pseudonym, Sir Charles. I am a self-taught graffiti artist and printmaker, and now I have a clothing brand that we use as a vessel to talk about internal issues going on in my neighborhood, in our communities. I grew up in the South Side of Chicago, Brighton Park area. Our alleyways were kind of like a gallery of graffiti, letter work, fonts and everything. We didn't have access to schools like the Institute of Design. This is how we grew up.

Further Reading:

Letters to Chicago by Sir Charles, published by Almighty & Insane Books

Compliments of Chicagohoodz by Jinx / Mr.C

I started a project maybe about eight years ago to start advocating about gang violence and mental health. This took me on a journey into a publication realm by doing a book, *Letters to Chicago*, with the Almighty & Insane publishing house from New York. This inner page (here on screen) is kind of a combination of street graffiti and this unique font for Chicago, which is a single line holding this letter word. I found this way of mixing both of them together to represent Chicago and also tell a story.

The city has been built to be very segregated. You have Hispanics in one area cut off by an expressway that separates Polish or Lithuanians from African-Americans. Because of the way the city has been so segregated, once they displace communities from their neighborhood, now they have to move into a new neighborhood. Because there's never been a dialogue, there's never been a communication, a lot of these youth that never really interacted with Hispanics or African-Americans decided to bond together and form their own groups, whether it was athletics clubs or baseball teams.

Installation view of *Letters Beyond Form: Chicago Types* at the Design Museum of Chicago, December 2024. Photo Credit: Ceninye Harris

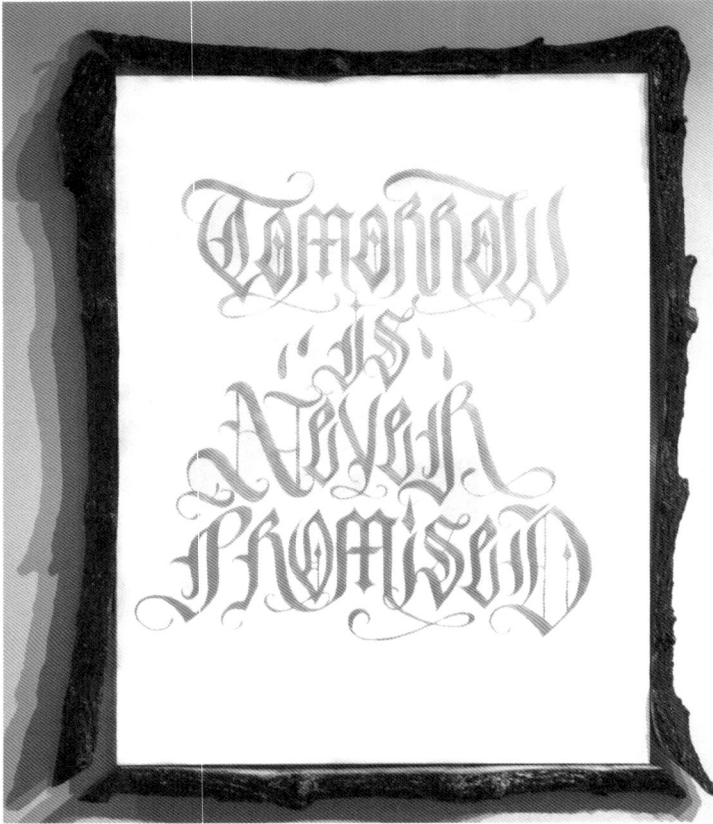

Amira: I know that you were previously involved in gang activity or around that a lot, and some of the lettering that you use is really related to gangs. How does that change or shape the way that you work?

Charlie: I joined a gang when I was pretty young, when I was 13, and this is how we communicated with each other. We communicated through letter work, through insignias, and that kind of became really rooted in our neighborhood. That's how we talk to each other. If you want to find out what's going on in the neighborhood, just look at the community, and you'll be able to tell if a neighborhood is going through a war between two different gangs, or who said it is, or who belongs there, or who's clean.

Because of this practice of tagging up walls and representing, it allowed me—now, in my current state— to use the same letterwork and imagery to talk about things like this moving forward.

My project started about eight years ago after a drive-by shooting at my daughter's school. I wanted to say something. I wanted to speak up. The best way that I knew was by utilizing this large spot to make work that

I know for sure is going to grab attention. One, because people are going to want to decipher it. What does this mean? What does it say? What are they trying to say? You know, what are they trying to tell?

I started doing graffiti back on the streets after this shooting. Sometimes I would write affirmations like "moving forward is not a betrayal", "learning how to forgive", all these positive things, because these are not things that are taught in certain households. Through the letter work, I communicate with my community using the same letter work, like the specific shape of the D or the M, the same symbols that they would recognize to kind of communicate with my neighborhood.

To use the letter work outside of what is normally utilized is very taboo. It's just taboo letter work, and this is my way of kind of rebelling against what was going on.

Amira: What really stands out to me about your work is how caring you are, how much it matters what you're doing. It's not just that you're designing because you need to make a living. You're not sort of making this transition, or even just using these letters because you think people will buy something. What is your process? How do you think through that moment of impact, the emotional receiving of your work knowing that you want to make something and putting it out into the world?

Charlie: A lot of these designs or drops that we do have an intention of either something happened, either something that I experienced, or something that the people that I work with have gone through. That becomes the motivation to create something. Whether we're going to sell one or not—that's the risk. We just want to put it out there. ∎

2031– 2034
(with future)

Chicago Tribune

Designing for Impact in the Built Environment

Elizabeth Blasius, Co-Founder, Preservation Futures
Katherine Darnstadt, Founding Principal, Latent

Preservation Futures is a Chicago-based firm exploring the future of historic preservation through research, action, and design. Latent is a progressive Chicago-based architecture firm working at the intersection of design and community development to create social, economic, and environmental impact. Together, Elizabeth and Katherine led a conversation about their approaches to designing and preserving the built environment with the goal of increasing justice, equity, and resiliency.

Elizabeth: I'm an architectural historian. I'm the co-founder of a preservation firm called Preservation Futures. We feel like preservation has a place in the future, even though it also has to do a lot with the way that the past is interpreted. Preservation functions as a practice, as a form of government, and as a form of activism.

We built our firm on advocating for a future for the James R. Thompson Center, built in 1985 and designed by Helmut Jahn. We really, really worked hard to make sure that the public understood how important the building was as a public building in Chicago. It was a center of protest and activism from 1985 up until just a few years ago when the state sold it to Prime Group and then to Google.

The building was instrumental in all these different ways that Chicagoans and people in Illinois talk to their government. It has an embedded history of protest and activism. The architecture in the building, the colors express all of that. We wrote a National Register of Historical Places nomination for the building. We advocated for the City of Chicago to landmark it. The City of Chicago had no interest in landmarking it at all. They didn't want to get into

The "Sbarro Urbanists" at the James R. Thompson Center. Image courtesy of Elizabeth Blasius

the state process that could interfere with selling the building. I've done a lot of work—a lot of writing—to bring out these other histories of the Thompson Center that aren't just about the architecture as the only important thing.

We also did a lot of silly shit. So this image on-screen is me and my business partner, Jonathan, and my friends Josh and Eric. We're part of a group of folks called the Sbarro Urbanists who would meet in the food court Sbarro at the Thompson Center and just eat pizza and enjoy the public space. We're a commercial firm that really just needed to have fun with the way that we work with advocacy and include as many people as possible.

Katherine: This is a fun fact. There are a lot of secret Sbarro Urbanists that were not part of this group in general. A lot of people met in that food court. I met my accountant for my business there. For many years, we would exchange paperwork and have a burger or Sbarro. For some reason we thought meeting in that food court was a good idea. That's where we met, and I got my taxes done with my accountant. We just liked it.

Elizabeth: So what's next in preservation? We need to figure out how to stop needlessly demolishing things at an ordinance level. The Chicago Historic Resources Survey and the Demolition Delay Ordinance are really not working, particularly in terms of vernacular housing. The kind of naturally growing affordable housing that is being demolished in Chicago is also historic housing. It's also historic buildings.

Whatever neighborhood you may live in, you may see that a lot of older buildings are being demolished for nothing, for a sidewalk. Maybe a multifamily building is being demolished for a single family home. That's something that we need to get a handle on.

We also need to figure out the architectural styles of the 70s, 80s, 90s. What are they? We need to figure out how to advocate for those. We need to recognize different types of preservation.

Katherine: I'm the founder of Latent. We're an architecture and urban design firm in Chicago. One of our projects is the Laramie State Bank site in the Austin neighborhood. While trying to preserve and repurpose it, the big building got better, and then it got worse. This example shows that even when a whole entire city is on board to preserve one particular building, how hard it is to actually get all the pieces together to make it work—from a timeline standpoint, from a financial standpoint, and then just a level of interest to continue throughout the project. Because one of the things that happens in these kinds of development models is you must start with letters of intents from tenants. But if the project takes four years, some of those tenants have opened up a shop somewhere else. So the timelines and the lives of these buildings have real impact.

Customer on the Fresh Moves Mobile Market bus. Image courtesy of Katherine Darnstadt

We are very much a design firm. We think about design excellence, but we also think about design activism within that same vein. We did an earlier project early in our career called Fresh Moves Mobile Market. It was a mobile produce market inside a decommissioned CTA bus. It still exists. We submitted it for a prestigious, larger-scale global design award, and we came in second. We were the runner-up. This (on the screen) is the comment one of the jurors said about our project. They said it was "a beautiful project, but might be too socio-political."

The comment was kind of rude, but also incredibly empowering, because this whole conference is about design and activism and saying, "Design is not neutral."

There are motivations and histories behind it, and it probably is political. Seeing that comment for the first time, somebody saying that we don't think your design is as powerful as the one that we chose because you thought about the context, the people, the issues of food deserts, all of these different things. That's why we dinged you. That's why you get silver and you don't get gold.

It's always been incredibly motivating to know that's the context we need to look at—that very large scale, whether it's food systems, preservation systems, corridor infrastructures, city policies—to start to think about the smallest element within those designed pieces.

That's the core of where our work has been the last 15 years. And hopefully 15 more. ∎

¡Anímate!: Values, Approaches, and Contexts in a Community-Based Arts Practice

Andrés Lemus-Spont & Marya Spont-Lemus, Co-creators, ¡Anímate! Studio

Since 2015, ¡Anímate! Studio has led 100+ free public workshops in neighborhoods on Chicago's South and Southwest Side. In this informal talkback, Andrés and Marya reflected on their approach of using art and design to explore values and build community power.

Andrés: Marya and I are ¡Anímate! Studio, and we've been doing this for almost 10 years. We do free public workshops in parks, plazas, and other public spaces. We use a lot of different materials. We like to think about it very playfully, with hands-on exercises in critical pedagogy, prompting questions around values reflected in objects and the surrounding world.

Marya: We're centering this session around values, relationships, approaches, and contexts—really thinking especially about the how and the why, and, of course, the who. Themes of personal exploration, collective play and agency, and building community power are at the heart of a lot of our work.

¡Anímate! in Spanish means, sort of like, "Go for it!" That's the main kind of vibe that we've taken on with it. When Andrés and I were choosing a name for the work we do together, he mentioned that it can often have an activist kind of usage. It's got this spirit of collective encouragement and going forward. Then there's *animate*, in English. It's not an identical meaning, but it still has this idea of movement towards action. So the name is mutually kind of intelligible, even if it doesn't have an identical meaning. We wanted to start there because that reflects some of our values of the work that we do together. Some of these shared values are community, mentorship, possibility and openness to experimentation, as well as encourage movement towards action.

Andrés: In the vein of this symposium and the idea of activism—

Our approach to activism is very much the idea of bringing the work that we do to people outside of institutionalized walls and into neighborhoods.

Especially people who might not otherwise seek out this work. One thing I want to point out is the idea of helping people discover what is already inside them. We very much think of it that way when we think about participants, that everyone can be creative and reflective. We can, as artists, create that space.

———————————————

Marya: There's not one right kind of partnership or one right kind of relationship. Sometimes a partnership can just be where you're cross-promoting something with somebody, and that's okay. Sometimes you're hosting somebody or inviting somebody into your space. But sometimes partnerships can be relationships with whole people that develop over years and years. They start somewhere and can keep growing. Partnerships are about trust-building, and also friendship-building. Like in this image on screen—we've been in all these people's houses, and they've been in ours. How do those evolve over time? Who are you on a shared journey with? Or, whose journey is aligning with your journey?

A FrankenToyMobile workshop as part of a Port Ministries community event in Back of the Yards, May 2016

"Finding Depths: Reflecting, Reframing, Responding on the River" workshop at Canalport Riverwalk Park, July 2023, presented as part of the Chicago Park District's Night Out in the Parks

I know the frame of this gathering is "Design as Activism." I think of the work that we do as generally closer to organizing than activism. They can definitely be interconnected. This is a moment where I think of organizing as being very, very, very much about relationships and activism. If we had this drum machine, and we just showed up to support a protest, I would think of that as activism. But doing it through this venue as part of this longer work, I think of that as organizing. ∎

How do your values, approaches, relationships, and context connect to make something uniquely yours?

Black-and-white photograph of people in conversation at a workshop; a man wearing glasses and holding a notebook gestures while speaking, with several attendees around him. The word "CONVERSATION" runs vertically down the left margin in large stylized letters.

Power Dynamics in Design Processes

Justin Walker, Business Strategy and Design Operations Lead,
   ChiByDesign
Sharon Bautista, Qualitative Research Manager, Code for America
Sharlene King, Strategy Designer and Innovation Consultant,
   Design, Salesforce

Power dynamics are always present in design projects. How much decision-making power should designers have? How can we structure projects to accommodate varying levels of involvement? This conversation explored different approaches to co-design and client engagement, focusing on clients' willingness to invest in capacity building and power-sharing. While most commercially viable projects tend to supplement power, there is potential for transformative power-sharing models.

Sharon: This conversation is about the connection between processes and methods we use and increasing power, amplifying power, shifting power, sharing power, and how we might leverage design processes to do that.

Sharlene: I'd be curious to know what aspect of design and power dynamics has the audience most concerned as you look into design as a practice.

Audience member: I think there's a misunderstanding about what design is and when it needs to be deployed. What are the components of design? For those of us that might work with people from other disciplines—being in healthcare as I am—it's how to advocate for the things that need to happen to find the solutions, to advocate for the solutions. A lot of people talk about process and things like that, and I find that that's lacking sometimes. In the discipline and as a designer, how do we do a good job advocating for those steps that we really need in order to arrive at a solution that's going to be successful?

"WHAT PART OF DESIGN PROCESS DESIGN METHODS?"

SHIFTING SHARING AMPLIFYING POWER

ADVOCATE for SOLUTIONS
ADVOCATE for STEPS

ASK "WHO YIELDS POWER DURING THE DESIGN PROCESS?"

CONVERSATION

SHARLENE KING

DESIGNERS as FACILITATORS CREATE CONDITIONS

POWER DYNAMICS of

"WHAT FORMS DOES POWER TAKE? HOW DOES IT SHOW UP?"

"DESIGN AS A FIELD NEEDS TO LEARN TO NOT GET IN IT'S OWN WAY"

JUSTIN WALKER

BUILDING RELATIONSHIPS IS IMPORTANT ASPECT OF SHARING POWER

"ARE YOU SHIFTING POWER OR ARE YOU RELINQUISHING IT?"

Conversation sketchnotes © Anushree Joshi (MDes + MBA 2026)

"FEELING LIKE SMALL FISH IN BIG POND WHEN VOICING OPINIONS"

"WE ALL ARE MEDIUM FISH"

TONE OF VOICE EXCHANGE WITH CLIENTS, TEAMS WITH RESPECT & KINDNESS

SHARON BAUTISTA

MAKE SPACE FOR GOOD INTERACTIONS IN WORKSPACES

DESIGN PROCESS

BREAKING CORPORATE TENSION

HOW COULD WE IMPROVE PROCESSES WHEN WORKING W CASEWORKERS?

HMW?

SHARE POWER WITH COMMUNITIES YOU ARE DESIGNING FOR.

"USING MY POWER TO FIGHT FOR, CASEWORKERS CAUSE"

BEING ACCOUNTABLE TO THE COMMUNITY

SKETCHNOTE BY: ANUSHREE JOSHI

DESIGN AS ACTIVISM ID

61

Justin: That's something that we deal with a lot. My experience may be a bit different because I'm more of a consultant. We have conversations with clients all the time around what we think needs to be done in a design process. We practice co-design. A lot of times, we run into clients who don't want to spend the money necessary to pay co-designers. Or, we know we will get into the conversation around what co-design is and how we find co-designers. A lot of times we may come into a situation where we typically hire co-designers onto our teams, and then we train them. But that takes time, so we have to advocate for that part of the process, because it's an important step. If there are parts of the process that you feel are absolutely necessary, you can't cut those steps.

You have to be comfortable enough to walk away if you think you're going to do a disservice to the folks who you're trying to help.

That can be a tough thing at times. I was just downstairs and heard a conversation around values and principles in this work. Especially working in social and civic design, you have to have some level, some floor where you say, "These are our values, these are our principles."

Sharlene: That's very different from what it is in the private sector. When we design, the user—the end person—is what we're focused on, making everything great for the client. But the people who hire designers, they're often beholden to other stakeholders that do not have that direct investment. When you have that kind of ecosystem, even the creative director or a designer are not going to have the same considerations, never mind the VP of your business or the Board Director of that VP. It keeps getting worse further up the ladder.

Sharon: In one project, I tried to use my power to amplify the voices of caseworkers in the state who could talk with me and share the problems with their workspaces with me. It came time to share our findings, and our main stakeholder shut me down. After that experience, basically I hit a wall. Then—not in a way to rile people up or try to defy the stakeholder, but as respectfully as I could—I told the other stakeholders I had met through interviews that I knew about these conditions. I shared these stories widely, as opposed to going to the governor. (I mean, I also did try to do that.)

I felt the way that I could use my power was to take the stories I had heard and just tell as many people as I could talk to in any role in the state that touched Human Services. Even though in that situation, I was pretty low on the ladder.

Sharlene: I wanted to talk about something similar. Something that other people mentioned is, especially as designers, we can get a superiority complex. We think of ourselves as smarter. But the reality is, when we talk about power dynamics, that's usually fed by anxiety.

We think about it as "big fish, little pond", and it's not like that. Actually, we're all like medium fishes. That's why we're so anxious.

We don't actually see who has the end power, except for someone like that, right? And so the only way to navigate that kind of power back to you is to start exerting pressure on the outside so that you shift the power. That's like one of the key things that's not so obvious to us.

When you threaten someone's power, you know when someone doesn't want to cede that power when they go to some base emotional responses. It may be coded in sophisticated jargon or policies, procedures, but at the end of the day, it's still that very basic emotional response of, "I need to protect what sustains."

Sara Cantor (as an audience member): I'll jump in just to continue the conversation about challenges with sharing power. For me a lot of it all comes down to is, who is accountable to whom? If I'm a designer and I work at a design firm, I am accountable to my clients. My client is maybe accountable to, in theory, the people they serve, but in practice, maybe more so, their board, their staff, their donors, etc. So we need to be accountable to our client. We also—I think more importantly—need to be accountable to community. This person is paying me, but this person is the person that I'm accountable to. That can sometimes be an inherent conflict, but not always. Of course, it's great if they're all on the same page and the work moves on.

Ultimately what we're trying to do by modeling how to be accountable to community, is to get our clients to be accountable to community.

I don't need to be in this transaction any longer, I can step away, but I want them to be in a place where they know how to do that. They know what that looks like. They felt it. They have a lived experience of, "Oh, this is how I should be operating this right." But it doesn't always work right, especially when you have, "Okay, well, client wants x, but community wants y."

Justin: In co-design, people create what it is that *they* want. It's not our job to say we know what the outcome should be. It's not our job necessarily to say we know what the intervention should be to get to the outcome. We try to create the conditions where people have the knowledge necessary, the tools necessary, the space necessary, to do what it is that they need to be done. I see a lot of instances in the design field where that's not happening, where we as designers come into the space and we have an idea of what needs to be done, and we just kind of run with it.

I've seen a lot of co-design work that really just brings people in to ask folks whether or not they think the ideas that are already presented make sense. But as designers, we have to take a step back and examine ourselves. A lot of the times we're driving towards outcomes that communities may not need. Instead, we're driving towards what *we* want to see in the world. To some degree, we have to bring our design politics to the process, but we also have to navigate that by allowing folks to show and tell us what needs to be created. ■

Exploring New Forms of Being

Rafa Robles, Co-founder, Director, Duo

In this conversation, Rafa discussed his design career trajectory, the formation and methodologies behind his studio, and a current project showcasing how Duo is creating new types of built environment interventions that benefit society.

Rafa: Currently in design spaces, there's this notion that you can only do so much, and you can only just work within the system that we're in. Societally or personally, as long as you do what you can within that world, then you're doing enough. But at Duo, we try to challenge that notion. That's a perspective that is often derived from, in a way, trauma, the designers' inability to do and to choose. Because a lot of the times we are taught to be good service providers. That's what we learn, how to service clients and how to service communities, and if you want to do more interesting work, you have to find better clients.

When I worked at an architecture firm, I got curious about where client requests were coming from. Why does a client want a 100-story tower and not an 80-story tower? And why a tower with the pool at the top and not a pool at the bottom? What is it?

Louis Sullivan has the saying "form follows function." We have to say, if architects or designers design the form, then who designed the function? We sort of learned to give that away and say, "The client designed the function. Unless somebody gives me the prompt as a designer, then I can't come up with it. I don't have permission to do that. I don't have the resources to do that. I'm not a developer. I'm not the owner of a company. Take your pick. I'm not a community member now."

We always have this tension where designers just give their power away. You don't even acknowledge it, but yet, you're the one creating all this stuff. So why? First and foremost, that's something that never really gets questioned.

Design thinking and human-centered design was very much at the service of capitalism. There is a very important thing to remember— that capitalism is not commerce.

It is not the same thing. Capitalism is not money. Those are not the same thing. Money is older than capitalism. Commerce is older than capitalism. But nowadays it's really trendy to talk about capitalism like it's the system that we're swimming in. People are like, "Well, I feel bad when I go to work because I make money and I'm capitalist." No, capitalism is controlling the systems of production in one particular thing and exploiting people and things and the environment for your benefit.

But even within those corporations there are so many things that you can do. There are so many paths you can chart within internally. There are paths you can chart externally. There are paths you can chart to work there for a few years, exit, and do something that you like.

My brother has a background in public policy. He worked at Deloitte and then was at Doblin in a similar group that I was in. We essentially got tired of the division between what we call *norm-making*, which is like strategy, policy, the invisible stuff in *form-making*, which is like design, art, architecture. We wanted to find a studio that does both, at the same time—*norming* and *forming*—one where you're actually bringing these idealized features into the world.

If I'm an immigrant, there are pretty big influences that drive my behavior. But usually immigrants don't design. We don't acknowledge, even those racist policies, histories, climates, all of the things that are currently happening. You have to sit here and question, why is the world so fucked up? Why, if there are so many people—like people in this conference— that are interested in making it better? Part of the answer lies in our training. We're not taught to have agency, so we feel like even if we have to go work for someone, we can't do something that we like on our own at the same time. Sometimes we don't have the privilege of doing that, but our lives are not singular.

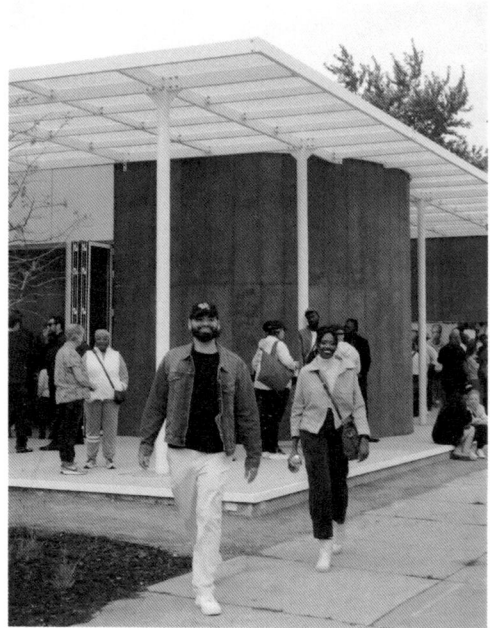

Starling project by Duo in North Lawndale, Chicago

At Duo we're imagining a new type of building that can be a neighborhood amenity, and then also share these profits with residents of the neighborhood. We conceptualized the Starling project as a space for liberation. In this building, what would a space for liberation be? We studied liberation. How can you achieve it? What do your people need?

A lot of times in design, we forget that our job is to make things up. It feels like a bad thing—"I made this up." Somehow we feel like we're not allowed to do that.

The exciting thing about design is that every single one of you possess your own form of self-expression. It would be great for all of you to find a way to let that out in whatever outlet you want, whether that is the built environment, designing ads, coming up with Bitcoin, doing whatever, like doing random drop cartoons. Some of my old coworkers became bakers—great bakers! ■

Multicontextualism is a design philosophy and creative approach for collective and self expression. It relies on recognizing the varied nested and interacting settings or venues (contexts) in which subjects, objects, environments, and influencing factors operate, and intentionally draws upon them to challenge preconceived norms and ideals to (re)create novel approaches to human life and explore new forms of being.

Rooted at the intersection of Norm-making (strategy/policy), and Form-making (design/art), Multicontextual Design calls for a fundamental shift in the ways interventions are designed and developed. It relies on defining and understanding boundary conditions (human, environmental, social, metaphysical, etc.), to then conceptualize and materialize new ideas into reality.

Multicontextualism promotes Norm / Form-making which enables us to (re)shape dominant norms and set new precedents through our work.

Founded in 2019 by brothers, Carlos Robles-Shanahan and Rafael Robles, Duo is an innovation studio/lab that pioneered Multicontextual Design to promote new possibilities for creative practice, craft interventions that improve collective quality of life, and explore new forms of being.

Designing Civic Imagination and Repair

Chandra Christmas-Rouse, Senior Associate, PolicyLin

Our democracy needs repair, and imagination must be part of the solution, says urban planner, systems designer, and artist Chandra Christmas-Rouse. In the closing keynote, Chandra unpacked how to design a future for our local democracies and cities, where we all belong. She shared her work in designing civic imagination and repair to create systems change and how designers can learn to practice imagination and repair in every space they're in.

I am an urban planner who was trained at a design school. For me, the power of design is about its ability to influence the relationship between people and their built environment. I think a lot about whose imagination has shaped our built environment and why and how we can expand our collective consciousness on what's possible in our built environment. How can we make visible power that is in part derived from being invisible? How can we help people to understand not only how we got here, but make a prescription about how we should think about where here is and provide some language for that?

This is not just a battle over who gets access to resources and cities, but it is also a battle of imagination.

As writer and scholar adrienne marie brown often reminds us, we are living in someone else's vision of who is deserving of these resources. I try to use the tool of design to interrupt that, to help order our attention and make us more literate in power so that ultimately we can get to a more nuanced understanding of how race and class in particular inform a very limited vision of our cities and how they continue to be shaped by those visions and what we can do to expand it.

Further Reading:

Loving Corrections by adrienne marie brown

Wayward Lives, Beautiful Experiments by Saidiya Hartman

My dad would take us on civic field trips all around the Washington, D.C. area. Sometimes it was to public libraries, sometimes it was to public school gyms, sometimes it was to college cultural centers. These are all places that we now see under attack, if we think about book bans and DEI initiatives across college campuses. I really believe this is part of what these spaces did for me and my dad and so many others. They trained us in imagination and empathy, which gets us to a place of repair.

Now I find us so polarized, because there's such few spaces left where we're around people or forced to be around people who are different from us and actually have to face their humanity and connect with them. In this moment, I believe we need to be trained in both imagination and repair. And you may be wondering, whose job is that?

My hope for today is that I can show you that it is the job of designers to train us in imagination and repair and most importantly, to get to the work of addressing our systemic inequities.

Listen to Chandra on the Scenic Roots and Climify podcasts:

Scenic Roots

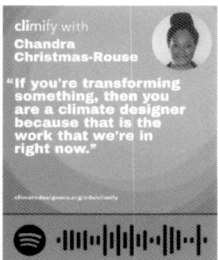

climify with Chandra Christmas-Rouse
"If you're transforming something, then you are a climate designer because that is the work that we're in right now."

When I worked at the Metropolitan Planning Council, we were constantly balancing between the subjectivity of culture and the objectivity of what we thought is just the policy and rationality that we're trying to do. So my job was to help these folks be nimble, to respond to this personal challenge.

We cannot disentangle policy analysis from cultural analysis, and we cannot ignore the relationships that are required to do this work, specifically to do this work well. So I wanted folks to understand how we're living into these roles so that we can navigate these systems differently and enable folks to be more self-aware about how they're functioning in these systems. We can build a culture to allow this work to sustain and take hold and think about themselves differently.

We had to think through the processes, the relational pieces of this that had to shift—not what's solely in your job description. Then this transformative work—what are the beliefs that we need to agree enough on to move this work forward, to not be perfectly in alignment or have everyone think exactly like us, but enough to be able to move the needle on this?

I hope this reinforces your belief that you do have the capacity to change and that we can create more lasting policy change. Generations of racist policies and decision-making have shaped the built environment that we see today. But it's up to us to decide what we will do about how our environments have been shaped based on the imagination and fears of very few people. How has that shaped our values and our beliefs along with it?

Where do we find the courage to take up that which has been handed to us by those like my dad, who was determined that the status quo was not sufficient? How do we transform ourselves into the fighters like you see my mom on screen—ready to take on the battle—who will sustain and keep building this movement of design as activism? How do we build the transformative relationships needed to make transformative solutions? Before we decide where we can go, we all need to know where we are, who we are, where we came from, and what we care about.

For me, it began with a spark on one of my dad's civic field trips and led to my career in designing civic imagination and repair. Those experience shapes not only our commitment to democracy, but also how we think change happens, who change is needed, for the acceptable methods of making that change, and what kind of change is possible. My time, my place, my community, my material conditions significantly shaped how I see the world, how I approach building a new one as we repair, and how I've come to think about change.

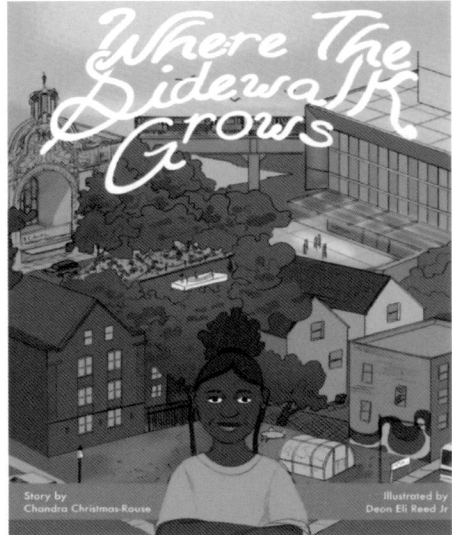

Where The Sidewalk Grows

Story by
Chandra Christmas-Rouse

Illustrated by
Deon Eli Reed Jr

This is my call for you all to engage more deeply with your imagination and to train others. I hope you answer this call. You can start today by envisioning a construction of a world not yet born, where more of our systems work for more people seek out the connections to help you construct it. Create those connections, those possibilities. It's all creative work.

While I share your fears, your furies, your righteous anger about this world and the work ahead, I also trust your creativity. You should, too.

Although this work will be messy, the possibilities on the other side will be worth it. I can't promise you what the resistance like what you often see in the media, but I can tell you that everyone in this space is our greatest hope. ∎